Baking *for* Christmas

Also by Maria Robbins

The Dumpling Cookbook
American Corn
Blue-Ribbon Cookies
Blue-Ribbon Pies
Blue-Ribbon Pickles and Preserves
A Cook's Alphabet of Quotations
The Christmas Companion (with Jim Charlton)
A Gardener's Bouquet of Quotations
Cookies for Christmas
Chili!

Baking *for* Christmas

Maria Robbins

———— ♦♦♦ ————

Illustrations by Durell Godfrey

ST. MARTIN'S GRIFFIN ❧ NEW YORK

Library of Congress Cataloging-in-Publication Data

Polushkin, Maria.
    Baking for Christmas / Maria Robbins.
        p.   cm.
    ISBN 0-312-13432-0 (pbk.)
    1. Christmas cookery. 2. Baking.   I. Title.
TX739.2.C45P65   1995
641.8'15—dc20   95-21292
                                                        CIP

First St. Martin's Griffin Edition: October 1995
10 9 8 7 6 5 4 3 2 1

◆ ◆ ◆

For Faith Hamlin, my agent; Barbara Anderson, my editor; and Joan Whitman, copy editor supreme. Thank you!

◆ ◆ ◆

Contents

Baking for
Christmas

MERRY VERY
BERRY
CHRISTMAS
CAKE
TO YOU!

For as long as I can remember, the anticipation of Christmas has been heightened for my sister and me by the prospect of receiving in the mail a package of cookies from our aunt Tamara. The most recent, I'm pleased to say, was this past December (and I am now in my fifties!). When we were young, her packages usually included other things as well—things she'd bought us with her hard-earned money: a toy, a sweater, pajamas. The store-bought things, as welcome as they were, made no lasting impressions on me. I can't recall even one of them in detail, even though as new arrivals to this country we lacked many of the amenities that Tamara's gifts provided. But the cookies were something else. She packed them in flat, rectangular department store gift boxes that she must have saved all year for the purpose, and I got to know the names of all the big stores in Manhattan long before I ever visited them. Best & Co., B. Altman, Saks Fifth Avenue, Gimbels, Lord & Taylor— I knew them all by their lovely, glossy white boxes, each with a different, swashy style of gold or embossed lettering. Tamara stuffed them with layers of wax paper, tissue paper, and cookies—dozens and dozens of wonderful cookies. In truth, she didn't have a large repertoire. One year there might be thimble cookies filled with raspberry jam, the next small round nut balls covered with confectioners' sugar, and the next perhaps sandwich cookies filled with apricot jam. The choices were random, and though my sister and I each had our favorites, we never told my aunt what they were; a rather limited element of surprise was part of the fun.

Today I send cookies and cakes and breads to my nephews, and the satisfactions are out of all proportion to the amount of labor involved. Both are convinced that I am the best cook in the whole world, and I do like to be the best at something. There's something utterly satisfying about homemade food as gifts. In an age that sometimes seems to have gone shamelessly commercial, it is a way of spending time and love instead of money on someone you care for. It pampers and coddles, and combines the flavors of home with a sense of caring that simply can't be reproduced in a commercial product. And it's a funny thing, but no matter how strict my diet might be at any given time, a homemade loaf of bread or fruitcake or box of cookies is always exempt from the day's calorie count.

In this book I've collected my favorite breads, cakes, and cookies for Christmas. Most are easy to make, none is difficult. Many can be made way ahead of time, and several actually improve with age, so that you can start preparations right after Thanksgiving. Best of all, if you are at all like me and detest the commercialization that attends this holiday, you can avoid the rush, the crowds, and the expense while you stay home surrounded by the lovely aromas and flavors of baking for Christmas.

A BAKING TIMETABLE

RIGHT AFTER THANKSGIVING:

1. Clear out as much space as possible in your freezer, so you have space to freeze breads, cakes, cookies, etc.
2. Make a list of your baking projects and their recipients. Collect the recipes and organize the list in terms of what should be baked first, to be frozen, aged, or mailed. Be realistic about your time and abilities.
3. Make a shopping list of ingredients and place orders for mail-order items.
4. Check your baking equipment and buy new items as necessary. I always

allow myself one special new item at the beginning of each Christmas baking season. This year I bought two more large cooling racks. Here's a quick checklist:

- parchment paper, wax paper, foil, plastic wrap, plastic food storage bags in a number of sizes, cellophane, paper doilies, and tissue paper
- baking pans, cookie sheets, cooling racks
- plastic containers with tight-fitting lids in a number of sizes, cookie tins, boxes, and cardboard cake rounds

FIRST WEEK OF DECEMBER

1. Start baking cookies, biscotti, fruitcakes, and items for the freezer.
2. Gather wrapping material and shipping cartons.
3. Gather packing material.
4. Gather labels and package sealing tape.

SECOND WEEK OF DECEMBER

1. Continue baking.
2. Start mailing packages for Christmas delivery.

THIRD WEEK OF DECEMBER

1. Continue baking like crazy.
2. Send packages you didn't send last week.

LAST DAYS BEFORE CHRISTMAS

1. Bake last-minute items for hand-delivered presents.

2. Package and wrap cookies, biscotti, and fruitcakes you baked three weeks ago.
3. Send packages by expensive delivery services because you didn't do it last week.
4. Bake at least one festive yeast bread for Christmas morning.

CHRISTMAS

Relax.

HOW TO PACK AND SHIP BAKED GOODS SO THEY ARRIVE IN GOOD CONDITION

1. Select the right container. Cookie tins, sturdy boxes with lids such as hat boxes, and plastic containers with tight-fitting lids are all excellent containers for shipping baked goods. Keep in mind that the container becomes part of the gift, so match the container to the person. A special friend might love a flowered hat box while a more practical one would be very happy with a large, reusable plastic container. (Somehow no kitchen ever has enough of these.) In a pinch, a sturdy cardboard box, such as those sold at post offices, will do very well.

2. Tissue paper and wax paper are your friends. Tissue paper provides insulation as well as a festive look. Insulate your container with several layers of tissue paper on the bottom and top, then layer wax paper between each layer of cookies, biscotti, or breadsticks. Close the container and use tape to secure the lid. Additional gift wrapping is up to you.

3. Protect your gift with the right mailing carton and packing material. The mailing carton should be made of heavy cardboard and be substantially larger than your gift package so that there is room for packing material to insulate the cake, bread, or cookies. There are lots of excellent packing materials around: crumpled newspaper is cheap and readily available; crumpled tissue paper is fine; popped (unbuttered) popcorn is excellent and biodegradable; styrofoam peanuts and bubble wrap are very effective, if ecologically unsound. Whatever you use, there should be several inches of packing material between all sides of the mailing carton and the package inside.

PACKAGING IDEAS FOR GIFTS DELIVERED
BY HAND

1. Make the wrapping as important as the gift. Collect baskets, tins, boxes, ribbons, and wrappings all year long, especially at yard sales, bazaars, flea markets, craft sales, and antiques shops. Some examples of unusual items:

- decorative cookie tins
- antique cookie jars
- large glass wide-mouthed jars with cork stoppers
- decorative plates and platters wrapped with colored cellophane
- Chinese food take-out containers lined with colored tissue paper
- pretty hat boxes lined with tissue paper
- woven baskets lined with tissue paper and wrapped with cellophane

2. Use dried flowers to decorate a Christmas wrapping. Almost any flower in your garden or florist's bouquet can be dried by hanging it upside down. Roses dry particularly well and are beautiful many months later, even when their color has faded.

3. For a gift to a fellow baker, include a special utensil: beautiful copper cookie cutters; a nutmeg grater with a supply of whole nutmeg; a kugelhopf pan; or even a set of heavy-duty wire cooling racks.

EQUIPMENT FOR BAKING

Electric mixer. Many recipes in this book call for a heavy-duty electric mixer. I find mine indispensable for mixing and kneading dough, creaming butter, and beating eggs.

Food processor. Some recipes call for the use of a food processor to chop nuts and to cut butter into dry ingredients.

Saucepan and double boiler. A heavyweight saucepan is needed to reduce syrups, and a double boiler is necessary for melting chocolate. If these are coated with a nonstick surface, all the better when it comes to cleaning up.

Measuring cups. You should have two kinds; one set of metal or plastic nesting cups with flat rims for dry ingredients, and glass measuring cups with a pouring spout and clear markings for liquid ingredients.

Measuring spoons. It is useful to have at least two sets of standard, graduated measuring spoons.

Mixing bowls. Have an assortment of large, medium, and small mixing bowls.

Wire whisk. Whisks are useful for blending flour with other dry ingredients, but if you don't have one you can use a fork.

Wooden spoons and rubber spatulas. Wooden spoons are used for hand mixing, and rubber spatulas for folding solid ingredients into a batter.

Rolling pin. A sturdy rolling pin is essential, and it is wise to invest in a heavy, hardwood rolling pin with ball bearing.

Cookie sheets. Use heavy-weight, shiny, metal cookie sheets. Avoid dark-colored baking sheets. Edges should be flat or barely turned up so that heat can reach cookies evenly from all directions. Insulated baking sheets are fine, but they will require a slightly longer baking time, usually the maximum baking time given in the recipe. Nonstick baking sheets are fine if they are made of heavy-weight metal and coated with a top-quality nonstick material. (If any of your baking sheets are light and flimsy, do yourself a favor and throw them out.) If you are short of cookie sheets and want to use a jelly roll pan, turn it upside down and use that side. Otherwise the raised edges will impede the flow of air to the cookies.

Baking pans. Other than cookie sheets you will need to have on hand the following baking pans:

- standard metal loaf pans measuring 9 × 5 × 3 inches, 8½ × 4½ × 2¾ inches (standard), 7½ × 3½ × 2 inches, and miniature loaf pans measuring 5 × 3 × 2⅛ inches.
- square baking pans measuring 9 × 9 × 2 inches and 8 × 8 × 2 inches
- a 9-inch round cake pan
- a 10-inch springform pan
- a kugelhopf mold
- a 10-inch tube pan

Baking parchment. An indispensable aid in my kitchen. It eliminates the need to grease cookie sheets or ever to clean them again. I dislike the parchment in rolls and buy it in sheets from Maid of Scandinavia or The King Arthur Flour Baker's Catalogue (see page 117). I find that I can use a sheet of parchment two or three times before discarding it. Aluminum foil (shiny side out) can be used instead of baking parchment in many recipes.

Oven thermometer. I've never found an oven that wasn't several degrees off, and an oven thermometer makes it possible for you to adjust the difference. Put the thermometer in the center of the oven when you turn it on. Wait 15 minutes to check the temperature and make the necessary adjustment. If the discrepancy is more than 50°F, you should have your oven calibrated.

Timer. The only time I have ever burned an entire batch of cookies was when I tried to do it without a timer. Set your timer to go off at the minimum baking time, so you can check the cookies and decide.

Wire cooling racks. Raised wire racks allow baked goods to cool quickly because the air reaches them from all directions.

Spatulas. You will find it useful to have several different kinds of spatulas. A narrow metal spatula is used for leveling dry ingredients and for loosening the edges of cookies, such as brownies or shortbread, from a pan. A wide, flexible metal spatula is used to remove baked cookies or biscotti from the baking sheets to a cooling rack. Rubber spatulas are used to scrape down the sides of a mixing bowl.

Strainers. Use a large metal strainer to strain confectioners' sugar and brown sugar to remove any lumps. Use a small, fine-meshed strainer for sifting confectioners' sugar over baked cakes, breads, and cookies and for straining lemon juice.

Brushes. Have a selection of brushes on hand for painting and decorating.

Plastic wrap. Very handy for wrapping doughs that need refrigeration before rolling out.

Storage containers and plastic food storage bags. These fall into two categories: ugly but useful, and pretty but useless for long-term storage. For storage at home I use the former—plastic containers with very tight lids. For gift wrapping and sending, I collect tins, boxes, baskets, etc.

INGREDIENTS

Flour. Unbleached all-purpose flour is called for in the great majority of the recipes. Measure flour by spooning it lightly into a measuring cup until it overflows, then level the top with the edge of a metal spatula or a knife. Do not tap the measuring cup to make the flour settle or try to press it in. Your measurement will not be accurate. Measure cake flour and cornmeal exactly the same way.

Butter. Please use only sweet (unsalted) high-fat-content butter (Land O Lakes is the best brand available in supermarkets across the country). Buy it in quantity and store it in the freezer.

Sugar. Granulated sugar is measured exactly like flour. Brown or light brown sugar is measured by pressing sugar down firmly until the cup is filled to the rim, then leveling with the edge of a metal spatula or a knife. Confectioners' sugar should be strained through a coarse sieve to remove any lumps, spooned lightly into a measuring cup, then leveled with the edge of a metal spatula or knife.

Eggs. Large eggs are called for in all recipes. Remove them from the refrigerator 30 minutes before using.

Nuts. Use unsalted nuts. Store all nuts in the refrigerator or freezer to prevent them from going rancid. Toasting nuts brings out their flavor and is called for in several recipes. To toast, preheat oven to 350°F. Spread the nuts in a single layer in a shallow baking pan. Bake until nuts are very hot and start to have a definite aroma, usually between 10 and 15 minutes. Let cool and remove any loose skin before using.

Nuts can be ground or very finely chopped in a food processor. I find it helps to add a tablespoon of sugar to keep them from becoming sticky. To coarsely chop nuts, a sharp long-bladed chef's knife is best.

Chocolate. Be sure to use the type of chocolate called for in the recipe, *i.e.*, unsweetened, bittersweet, or semisweet, and use the best quality you can find.

Cocoa. Use the type of cocoa called for, usually an unsweetened cocoa powder.

Vanilla extract and other flavorings. In any recipe calling for vanilla or almond extract or any other extract flavoring, please use the ones that are labeled "pure extract" and avoid any with the word "imitation" on the label.

Oatmeal. Always use plain rolled oats (sometimes called "old-fashioned oats"), not the quick-cooking or instant type.

Cookies

• LEBKUCHEN •

I love to try new cookies during my Christmas baking, but there are a handful of traditional cookies that always get included. Lebkuchen are my absolutely all-time favorite Christmas cookies. To me they are what gingerbread promises, but never delivers. Best of all, you can make them way ahead of time, because they only improve with age.

All over Germany there are many variations on this old and very traditional Christmas cookie. Most of them include candied orange or lemon peel and citron. In this recipe I've replaced these with golden raisins and candied ginger. Ginger, it seems, is not usually included in Lebkuchen, but I think that it makes a spectacular addition.

4 cups unbleached all-purpose flour
½ teaspoon baking soda
½ teaspoon baking powder
½ teaspoon salt
1 teaspoon ground cinnamon
½ teaspoon crushed aniseed
½ teaspoon ground cardamom
¼ teaspoon nutmeg
¼ teaspoon ground cloves
1 cup ground toasted almonds
1 cup chopped toasted almonds
¾ cup honey

¾ cup brown sugar
½ stick (4 tablespoons) unsalted butter
Grated zest of 1 orange, preferably organic
Grated zest of 1 lemon, preferably organic
¼ cup brandy, Cognac, or bourbon whiskey
2 large eggs
½ cup finely chopped golden raisins
½ cup finely chopped candied ginger (optional)

For the glaze:
1½ cups sifted confectioners' sugar
3 tablespoons fresh lemon juice

1. In a large bowl and using a whisk, blend together flour, baking soda, baking powder, salt, cinnamon, aniseed, cardamom, nutmeg, and cloves. Stir in the almonds and set aside.

2. In a medium-size saucepan, cook the honey, brown sugar, and butter over medium heat, stirring constantly, until the butter melts and the sugar dissolves. Pour into the bowl of an electric mixer. Stir in the orange zest, lemon zest, and brandy and let the mixture cool.

3. Using the paddle on your mixer, beat in the eggs, one at a time, until each is completely absorbed. Lower the speed and stir in the raisins and candied ginger. Stir in the flour mixture, adding it ½ cup at a time.

4. Remove the dough to a lightly floured surface and knead it briefly until smooth and elastic. Divide the dough in half and pat each piece of dough into a rectangle about ½ inch thick. Wrap tightly in plastic wrap and refrigerate for at least 2 days or for as long as 5 days. This allows the flavors to mellow and ripen.

5. Preheat oven to 350°F. Line 2 to 4 baking sheets with parchment paper.

6. Roll out each piece of dough on a lightly floured surface into a large (15- by 9-inch) rectangle ¼ inch thick. Cut the dough into 36 (1½- by 2½-inch) rectangles, cutting 6 strips each way. Arrange the cookies 1 inch apart on the prepared baking sheets.

7. Bake one sheet at a time for 15 minutes—a few minutes less if you like very soft cookies and a few minutes more if you like them very hard. Cool on wire racks.

8. Prepare the glaze: In a small bowl, stir the confectioners' sugar with the lemon juice until smooth. Spread the glaze on the lebkuchen while they are still slightly warm.

9. Store the cooled cookies in an airtight container for at least 2 weeks and for as long as 2 months.

Yield: 6 dozen cookies

When I was a girl, preparations for Christmas started in early September when we children gathered black walnuts, hickory nuts, and hazelnuts. Hazelnuts grew along the edge of the woods on low bushes, but hickories and black walnuts grew on tall trees, and so we had to wait until they fell to the ground before racing with the squirrels to collect them. The black walnuts and hickory nuts were gathered early in autumn to give them time to dry out in the sun: If they were not dry, it was almost impossible to crack their tough inner shells. We'd wedge an upturned flatiron between our knees, put a dried nut on the hard surface, and take a hammer to it. Using a nut pick or sometimes a hairpin we'd pry the nut meats from the shell—rich, flavorful nut meats that even on those warm, bright days, filled us with happy anticipation because we knew they would be baked into Christmas cakes and cookies.

—Edna Lewis

• CHOCOLATE-DIPPED LACE COOKIES •

These are very dressy cookies. They will keep for about ten days, layered between sheets of wax paper in an airtight container.

1 stick (¼ pound) unsalted butter
1 cup finely chopped almonds
1 cup rolled oats (not instant or
  quick cooking)
⅔ cup sugar
1 large egg, beaten

1 tablespoon all-purpose flour
½ teaspoon baking powder
2 tablespoons milk
For dipping:
6 squares semisweet chocolate, melted
  and kept warm in a double boiler

1. Preheat oven to 400°F. Line a baking sheet with foil and spray with nonstick vegetable spray. Cut three more sheets of foil and spray them with nonstick vegetable spray.

2. In a medium saucepan, melt the butter over low heat. Remove pan from heat and stir in ½ cup of the chopped almonds, then all of the oats, sugar, egg, flour, baking powder, and milk.

3. Drop the batter by teaspoonfuls onto the prepared baking sheet. Leave 3 inches between each drop because these cookies will really spread when they bake.

4. Bake the cookies for 4 to 7 minutes, or until the edges turn a light brown color. (While the cookies are baking, drop the remaining batter onto the waiting foil sheets.) Remove cookies from the oven and slide the foil onto a countertop to let the cookies cool until you can peel the foil away from their bottoms. Transfer the cookies to a wire rack and cool completely.

5. Slide another sheet of foil with cookie batter on it onto the cookie sheet and bake as above.

6. When all the cookies are cool and quite firm, dip half of each cookie into the melted chocolate and then into a small bowl of the remaining chopped almonds. Cool on wire racks until the chocolate hardens.

Yield: about 4 dozen cookies

• CINNAMON ALMOND BARS •

These pure almond cookies are sparked with the flavors of cinnamon, lemon, and vanilla. Store them in an airtight container and they will keep for a very long time.

1 cup blanched whole almonds
½ cup sugar
8 ounces canned almond paste
1 large egg white, at room
  temperature
½ teaspoon ground cinnamon
Grated zest of 1 lemon

1 teaspoon vanilla extract
A handful of all-purpose flour for
  dusting the work surface
For the glaze:
1 egg white, lightly beaten
½ cup slivered almonds

1. Preheat oven to 350°F. Line a baking sheet with parchment paper.

2. Spread the blanched almonds on a cookie sheet and toast them in the oven for 10 to 15 minutes. Remove from oven and spread them on paper towels. Let cool to room temperature.

3. Reduce oven temperature to 300°F.

4. Place the almonds and ¼ cup of the sugar into the bowl of a food processor outfitted with a steel blade. Pulse just until the almonds are in small chunks.

5. Transfer to the bowl of a heavy-duty mixer equipped with a paddle attachment. Add the remaining ½ cup of sugar, the almond paste, and the egg white. Mix at very low speed, adding the cinnamon, lemon zest, and vanilla extract until well blended.

6. Remove the dough to a lightly floured surface. It will be firm but a little sticky. Sometimes it helps to rub your hands with flour. Pat the dough into a rectangle about 6 inches wide and 10 inches long. Cut the dough into bars that are 2 inches long and 1½ inches wide. Set the cookie bars on the prepared baking sheet. Brush the tops with the egg white and sprinkle with the slivered almonds.

7. Bake for 20 to 25 minutes, until the cookies turn a light golden color. Use a spatula to remove the cookies to a wire rack and cool completely.

Yield: about 20 cookies

. . . the raisins were so plentiful and rare, the almonds so extremely white, the sticks of cinnamon so long and straight, the other spices so delicious, the candied fruits so caked and spotted with molten sugar as to make the coldest lookers-on feel faint and subsequently bilious. Nor was it that the figs were moist and pulpy, or that the French plums blushed in modest tartness from their highly decorated boxes, or that everything was good to eat and in its Christmas dress. . . .

—Charles Dickens

• HAZELNUT HONEY BROWNIES •

I found the original of this recipe in Beatrice Ojakangas's *Great Holiday Baking Book* (New York: Clarkson N. Potter, Inc., 1994). I've made it many times, experimenting with different nuts (she calls for walnuts or pecans) and honey gathered from many different flowers. The honey not only keeps these brownies moist and chewy, but also adds its own subtle flavor. Currently I've been using a leatherwood honey from Tasmania (I found it on the shelves of my grocery store) and I think it makes the best brownies. But I felt exactly the same way with all the other honeys I've tried.

1½ cups hazelnuts
½ cup all-purpose flour
⅓ cup dark, unsweetened cocoa
½ teaspoon salt
6 tablespoons unsalted butter, at
  room temperature
½ cup sugar
½ cup flavorful, aromatic honey

2 large eggs
2 teaspoons vanilla extract
For the frosting:
1 cup confectioners' sugar
2 tablespoons dark, unsweetened cocoa
2 tablespoons fresh orange juice or
  water
1 teaspoon vanilla extract

1. Preheat oven to 350°F. Spray a 9-inch square baking pan with nonstick vegetable spray.

2. Spread the hazelnuts on a cookie sheet and toast them for 10 to 15 minutes in the oven, until they start to release a wonderful aroma. Remove them from the oven and cool until you can handle them. Rub the hazelnuts together between your hands to remove some of the brown skins. Most of

the skin should come off easily; don't worry about the bits that don't. Spread the nuts on a cutting board and chop coarsely with a chef's knife. Set aside.

3. Combine the flour, cocoa, and salt in a bowl and stir with a wire whisk to blend.

4. In another bowl, cream the butter with an electric mixer at medium speed. Raise speed to high and gradually beat in the sugar and honey. Continue beating until the mixture is light and fluffy. Beat in the eggs, one at a time, and vanilla extract until completely incorporated.

5. Stir in the flour and cocoa mixture and mix until smooth. Stir in the hazelnuts.

6. Pour the batter into the prepared pan and bake for 25 to 30 minutes. Be careful not to overbake. The cake should be set but still moist in the center. Remove from the oven and cool in the pan on a wire rack.

7. When the brownies are completely cooled, mix the confectioners' sugar, cocoa, orange juice, and vanilla in a small bowl until smooth. Spread the frosting over the cake and cut it into squares. The brownies will keep in the refrigerator for 1 week, or in the freezer for several months.

Yield: 12 brownies

• MAPLE SUGAR COOKIES •

These cookies hail from our northern neighbors in Quebec province, where maple sugar is probably more easily available than it is to a writer on the eastern tip of Long Island. Thanks to the convenience of mail order, however, cooks anywhere can make these wonderful cookies. The maple sugar imparts a subtle and haunting flavor that makes the cookies irresistible.

3 cups unbleached white flour
1 teaspoon baking soda
½ teaspoon salt
½ stick (4 tablespoons) unsalted butter, at room temperature

1 pound maple sugar, crushed (2 cups)
2 large eggs
1 teaspoon vanilla extract
1 cup sour cream

1. In a small bowl, stir the flour, baking soda, and salt with a wire whisk, to blend.

2. In the bowl of an electric mixer, cream the butter and maple sugar together at medium speed until smooth. Beat in the eggs, one at a time, and the vanilla extract until light and fluffy.

3. Add the sour cream and beat on low speed until well blended. Gradually beat in the flour mixture to make a smooth, medium-soft dough. Remove the dough to a sheet of plastic wrap and press the dough into a flat round disk. Wrap well and chill in the refrigerator for 2 hours.

4. Preheat oven to 375°F. Line cookie sheets with parchment paper.

5. Turn the dough out onto a lightly floured surface and roll it out to a thickness of ⅛ inch. Cut into rounds with a 2-inch round cookie cutter and set on prepared baking sheets, about 1 inch apart.

6. Bake for 10 to 12 minutes, until cookies are golden brown. Remove from oven and transfer cookies to wire racks to cool. Let cool completely, then store the cookies in an airtight container where they will keep for up to 2 weeks.

Yield: about 50 cookies

· PARSONS' HATS ·

These delicious cookies (*Pfaffenhütchen*) come from Germany via a friend's retired nanny. I don't know if they are particularly associated with Christmas, but I know that they are unusual, and anyone who is lucky enough to get these as a gift (they tend to want to stay at home where they've been made) always wants more.

1 cup hazelnuts, roasted, peeled,
    and ground into a meal
⅔ cup sugar
1 cup unbleached white flour
½ teaspoon baking powder
6 tablespoons unsalted butter, at
    room temperature

1 large egg
½ teaspoon grated lemon peel
1 cup blanched almonds, ground into
    a meal
1 egg yolk, lightly beaten with 1
    tablespoon water

1. Preheat oven to 400°F. Line a baking sheet with parchment paper.

2. Prepare the filling: In a medium bowl, mix together the ground hazelnuts and ⅓ cup sugar with enough water to make a creamy mixture that holds together and set aside.

3. In a medium-size bowl, stir the flour and baking powder with a wire whisk, to blend.

4. In a large bowl, cream the butter with an electric mixer at medium speed. Increase the speed and gradually beat in the remaining ⅓ cup of sugar. Continue beating until the mixture is light and fluffy. Beat in the egg and lemon peel, reduce speed, and beat in the ground almonds.

5. Fold in the flour mixture to make a dough. Remove the dough to a lightly floured surface and roll it out to a thickness of ¼ inch. Cut the dough into 3-inch rounds with a cookie cutter. Place a small amount (about ½ teaspoon) of the hazelnut mixture in the center of each round, draw up the edges, and pinch them together. Place the cookies on the prepared cookie sheet, about 1 inch apart, and brush them with the egg yolk mixture.

6. Bake in the center of the oven for 15 minutes, or until lightly browned. Remove from the oven and transfer the cookies to a wire rack to cool. Store completely cooled cookies in airtight containers where they will keep for up to 2 weeks.

Yield: 2 dozen cookies

• CHOCOLATE CHERRY OATMEAL COOKIES •

These are hearty, soul-satisfying cookies that are a great favorite with anyone who tries them. They are not at all fragile, which means they are perfect for shipping to faraway friends and family, who will think of you with every delicious bite.

1½ cups unbleached all-purpose
flour
1 teaspoon baking soda
½ teaspoon salt
2 sticks (½ pound) unsalted butter,
at room temperature
½ cup granulated sugar
½ cup firmly packed brown sugar

3 large eggs
1 teaspoon vanilla extract
2 cups rolled oats (not instant or quick
cooking)
1 12-ounce bag semisweet chocolate
chips
1 cup dried cherries
Granulated sugar for topping

1. Preheat oven to 375°F. Line cookie sheets with parchment paper.
2. Whisk together the flour, baking soda, and salt in a small bowl.
3. Cream the butter in the large bowl of an electric mixer at low speed for about 5 minutes. Raise the speed to high and gradually pour in the granulated sugar, beating for 2 to 3 minutes. Do the same for the brown sugar. Beat in the eggs, one at a time, and the vanilla extract, blending well after each addition.
4. Turn the mixer to low and stir in the dry mixture to make a smooth batter. Stir in the oats, chocolate chips, and dried cherries.
5. Drop tablespoonfuls of dough onto the cookie sheets, leaving at least

3 inches of space all around. Flatten each cookie with the bottom of a water glass dipped in granulated sugar.

6. Bake the cookies until the edges turn golden brown and the cookies are just set, about 12 minutes. Transfer the cookies to wire cooling racks and cool completely before storing them in airtight containers, where they will keep for up to 1 month at room temperature.

Yield: about 4 dozen cookies

Some say that ever 'gainst that season comes
Wherein our Saviour's birth is celebrated,
The bird of dawning singeth all night long;
And then, they say, no spirit can walk abroad;
The nights are wholesome; then no planets strike,
No fairy takes, nor witch hath power to charm,
So hallow'd and so gracious is the time.
　　　　　　　　　　—Hamlet, Act I, Scene I

• ROSE-SCENTED COOKIES •

These crumbly, delicate cookies resemble Mexican wedding cake cookies in texture, but they are fragrant with the taste of almonds and roses, a heavenly combination.

In my garden, I grow a few roses that don't need (or, in any case, don't get) any spraying, and over the summer I collect and dry rose petals. At Christmastime, I like to package and serve these cookies arranged on a bed of rose petals.

1 cup whole almonds
1 stick (¼ pound) unsalted butter,
   at room temperature
¼ cup confectioners' sugar
1½ tablespoons rose water

¼ teaspoon salt
½ cup unbleached all-purpose flour
½ cup whole wheat pastry flour
Confectioners' sugar for finishing the
   cookies

1. Preheat oven to 350°F. Spread the almonds on a baking sheet and toast them for 8 to 10 minutes. Remove from the oven and spread them on paper towels to cool. Turn off the oven.

2. Process the cooled almonds in a food processor to a fine meal and set aside.

3. In the bowl of an electric mixer, cream the butter and sugar at medium speed until light and fluffy. Beat in the rose water and almond meal. Reduce mixer speed to low and stir in the salt and flour, adding it about ¼ cup at a time. Remove the dough, wrap it in plastic wrap, and refrigerate for at least 3 hours or up to 12 hours.

4. Preheat oven to 350°F. Line a baking sheet with parchment paper.

5. Pinch off small pieces of dough and shape into balls about 1 inch in diameter. Arrange the balls about 1 inch apart on the baking sheet and bake for about 15 minutes, until the cookies are just starting to turn a golden color. Let them cool briefly on the baking sheet, roll in confectioners' sugar, and cool on wire racks. Roll in sugar again before storing in an airtight container. The cookies will keep for up to 2 weeks.

Yield: 2 dozen cookies

• LEMON SQUARES ON A CHOCOLATE CRUST •

Everybody I know loves lemon squares out of all proportion to how easy they are to make. They are one of the most popular desserts I serve. So I was totally thrilled when my cousin in Maine sent me this recipe for lemon squares sitting on a chocolate crust. A heavenly combination of flavors.

For the crust:
1 cup unbleached all-purpose flour
¼ cup confectioners' sugar
3 tablespoons cocoa powder
1 stick (¼ pound) cold unsalted
   butter
¼ cup ground walnuts

For the top layer:
2 large eggs
¾ cup granulated sugar
¼ cup fresh lemon juice
1 teaspoon grated lemon rind
2 tablespoons unbleached all-purpose
   flour
½ teaspoon baking powder
2 tablespoons confectioners' sugar

1. Preheat oven to 350°F.

2. Prepare the crust: Combine flour, confectioners' sugar, and cocoa in the bowl of a food processor fitted with a metal blade. Pulse on and off to blend. Cut the butter into small pieces and add it together with the ground walnuts. Process the mixture until it resembles coarse meal.

3. Pat the mixture into the bottom of an 8-inch-square metal pan and bake for 15 minutes to set the crust.

4. Prepare the top layer: In the bowl of an electric mixer, beat the eggs at medium speed until they turn a light color. Beat in the sugar gradually

until the mixture is thick and pale. Beat in the lemon juice and lemon rind. Sift the flour and baking powder over the egg mixture and stir it in to blend. Pour the egg mixture over the chocolate crust and bake for 20 to 25 minutes, until the topping is set. Remove from the oven and sift the confectioners' sugar over the top. Cool on a wire rack to room temperature and refrigerate for at least 1 hour before cutting into 1-inch squares. These will keep in an airtight container for 1 week.

Yield: 16 squares

The first rule in buying Christmas presents is to select something shiny. If the chosen object is of leather, the leather must look as if it had been well greased; if of silver, it must gleam with the light that never was on sea or land. This is because the wariest person will often mistake shininess for expensiveness.

—P.G. Wodehouse

• ZIMSTERNE: CINNAMON CHRISTMAS STARS •

These unusual Christmas cookies from Germany contain no flour, butter, or egg yolk. They are as light and ethereal as the stars they represent, and make a nice switch from all the other rich goodies that abound at Christmastime. They make a perfect gift for someone on a low-fat diet.

6 large egg whites
3 cups superfine sugar
¼ teaspoon salt
2 teaspoons grated lemon zest

2 teaspoons ground cinnamon
1 pound (about 4 cups) almonds,
*   finely ground*

1. In the bowl of an electric mixer, beat the egg whites at medium speed until soft peaks form. At high speed, gradually beat in the sugar and salt until the egg whites form very stiff and glossy peaks. Measure 1 cup of the meringue and set aside. Beat the lemon zest and cinnamon into the remaining meringue, then carefully fold in the almonds.

2. Turn out the meringue onto a lightly floured surface that has been sprinkled with granulated sugar. Use a rubber spatula to spread out the meringue until it is about ½ inch thick. Let it stand, uncovered, for 30 minutes.

3. Preheat oven to 350°F. Line two baking sheets with parchment paper.

4. Dust a rolling pin with flour and roll out the meringue to a ¼-inch thickness. Use a star-shaped cookie cutter, about 3 inches wide, to cut out stars, arranging them on the prepared cookie sheet about 1 inch apart. Gather the scraps and roll them out again to cut out more stars. Use a

small brush (an artist's brush is best) to paint the tops with the reserved meringue.

5. Bake one sheet at a time for 15 minutes, until the stars are firm and dry. Cool them on wire racks and store in an airtight container for up to 1 week. They can be frozen for up to 3 months.

Yield: 2 dozen cookies

• KOURABIEDES:
GREEK WALNUT CHRISTMAS COOKIES •

My family emigrated to this country in 1949 when I was eight years old. Until I moved away to my own apartment in New York City, we lived in Queens. Shortly after we moved to Queens, a Greek family, newly arrived in this country, moved into the apartment above us. While all of us struggled to learn our new language, the language of cooking and celebration presented no problem at all. On our very first Christmas in this country, Mrs. Demetro presented us with a plate of these crumbly, melt-in-your-mouth cookies. Each cookie is studded with a clove to represent the spices that were brought to the Christ child by the Three Kings. So many years later, these are still among my favorite cookies to make and give as Christmas presents.

2 cups unbleached all-purpose flour
½ teaspoon baking powder
¼ teaspoon salt
1 cup ground toasted walnuts
2 sticks (½ pound) unsalted butter,
   at room temperature

½ cup granulated sugar
1 egg yolk
1 tablespoon brandy or Cognac
1 teaspoon vanilla extract
72 whole cloves (optional)
2 cups confectioners' sugar for topping

1. In a medium-size mixing bowl, whisk together the flour, baking powder, salt, and walnuts and set aside.

2. In the bowl of an electric mixer, cream the butter and sugar until light and fluffy. Beat in the egg yolk, brandy, and vanilla extract. Stir in the flour mixture ½ cup at a time, blending well after each addition. Cover and refrigerate the dough for 1 hour.

3. Preheat oven to 350°F. Line 2 baking sheets with parchment paper.

4. Roll teaspoonfuls of dough into 1-inch balls. Stick a clove into each ball and arrange the balls on the prepared cookie sheets, about 1 inch apart.

5. Bake the cookies for 15 to 18 minutes, until they are lightly browned and firm to the touch. Spread 1 cup of the confectioners' sugar in a jelly roll pan or baking sheet with a rim. Remove the cookies to the sugar-lined pan. Sift the remaining confectioners' sugar over the cookies and roll them around to coat them completely with the sugar. Remove to wire racks to cool. Store them in an airtight container for up to 2 weeks or freeze for up to 3 months.

Yield: about 6 dozen cookies

Rings and jewels are not gifts, but apologies for gifts. The only gift is a portion of thyself.

—Ralph Waldo Emerson

◆ CHOCOLATE PRETZELS ◆

The pretzel shape has special significance at Christmastime. It comes from an ancient calendar symbol used to mark the winter solstice. Originally it was a circle, representing the orbit of the sun, with a dot in the center, representing the earth. When it was translated into dough, the dot first became a cross, and as bakers increasingly formed the shape from a single piece of rolled dough, the design became even more stylized and assumed the shape we know today.

These amusing and delicious cookies simulate the look of traditional salt-covered pretzels and make a very attractive and popular gift.

1⅔ cups flour
⅓ cup unsweetened cocoa
2 teaspoons powdered instant coffee
¼ teaspoon salt
1½ sticks (12 tablespoons) unsalted butter

¾ cup granulated sugar
1 teaspoon vanilla extract
1 large egg white, slightly beaten
2 tablespoons pearl sugar or crushed sugar cubes

1. In a medium-size bowl, whisk together the flour, cocoa, coffee, and salt. Set aside.

2. In the bowl of an electric mixer, cream the butter, sugar, and vanilla extract until light and fluffy. On low speed, gradually blend in the flour mixture until just incorporated. Gather dough into a ball, wrap well in plastic wrap, and refrigerate for 1 hour.

3. Preheat oven to 350°F. Line several baking sheets with parchment paper.

4. Divide dough into four parts. Work with one part at a time, keeping the rest refrigerated. Divide each portion of dough into 8 equal pieces. Dust your hands with flour and with your palms roll each piece into an 8-inch-long strand. Twist each strand into a pretzel shape. Place 1 inch apart on prepared cookie sheets.

5. Brush each cookie with beaten egg white and sprinkle coarse sugar over the surface.

6. Bake for 12 to 14 minutes, until cookies feel just firm when lightly touched. Remove from oven and let cool on cookie sheets for a minute or two. Transfer cookies to wire racks to cool. Store completely cooled cookies in a tightly covered container, where they will keep for 2 weeks. Freeze them for up to 3 months.

Yield: 32 chocolate pretzels

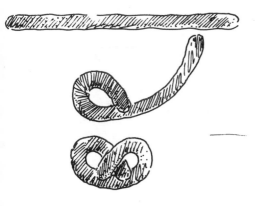

• BUTTERSCOTCH BROWNIES •

Whether you call them blondies or brownies, these buttery, chewy, melt-in-your-mouth bars are easy to make and make a great gift, either all by themselves or in an assortment of other cookies.

1 cup unbleached all-purpose flour
1 teaspoon baking powder
Pinch of salt
5 tablespoons unsalted butter

1 cup firmly packed light brown sugar
1 large egg, lightly beaten
1 teaspoon vanilla extract
½ cup chopped toasted walnuts

1. Preheat oven to 350°F. Butter a 9-inch square pan, dust with flour, and knock out the excess.

2. In a medium-size bowl, whisk together the flour, baking powder, and salt.

3. In a medium-size saucepan, melt the butter over medium heat. Add the brown sugar and stir until the sugar dissolves. Remove from heat and let cool for about 5 minutes.

4. Beat in the egg and vanilla. Gradually stir in the flour mixture until blended, then stir in the walnuts.

5. Spread the batter in the prepared pan. Bake for 20 to 25 minutes, just until the center is firm to the touch. Remove from the oven and place the pan on a wire cooling rack. Let stand for 10 to 15 minutes, then cut into 1½-inch squares. Remove from pan when entirely cool. Store in an airtight container for up to 1 week or freeze for up to 3 months.

Yield: 36 1½-inch squares

Biscotti

• ALMOND TOFFEE BISCOTTI •

I adapted this recipe from one I found in an afternoon of poking around on the Internet. It had no attribution and so I sent my thanks into cyberspace for it has become one of my favorites. The little toffee bits are delightful to encounter in these very chewy biscotti. You will probably find toffee bits in the same section as chocolate chips in the baking section of your supermarket.

3½ cups all-purpose flour
1 tablespoon baking powder
Pinch of salt
1 stick (¼ pound) unsalted butter,
  at room temperature
1 cup granulated sugar
5 large eggs

1½ teaspoons vanilla extract
½ teaspoon almond extract
1½ cups almonds, toasted
1 cup toffee bits
Topping:
1 large egg white, slightly beaten
⅓ cup granulated sugar

1. In a medium-size bowl, whisk together the flour, baking powder, and salt.

2. In the bowl of an electric mixer, beat the butter and sugar at medium speed until light and fluffy. Beat in eggs, one at a time, then beat in the vanilla and almond extracts.

3. With mixer on low speed, gradually beat in the flour mixture until well blended. Stir in nuts and toffee. Divide the dough into thirds, wrap each piece in plastic wrap, and refrigerate about 3 hours, until firm.

4. Preheat oven to 350°F. Line 2 baking sheets with parchment paper.

5. On a lightly floured surface, shape each portion of dough into a

12-inch log, about 2 inches in diameter. Place two of the logs 4 inches apart on one of the cookie sheets and the third log on the other. Brush the logs with egg white, then sprinkle with sugar.

6. Bake 30 to 35 minutes, until the logs feel firm and have colored to a light gold. The tops will start to show some cracks.

7. Remove from oven (leave the oven on) and place the cookie sheets on wire racks. Loosen logs with a wire spatula and let cool for 10 minutes.

8. Slide baked logs onto a cutting board. With a long serrated knife, cut each log diagonally into ½-inch slices. Arrange the biscotti, cut side down, on the cookie sheets. Bake 12 to 15 minutes, turning the biscotti over once, until dry and toasted a light golden color. Remove the biscotti to a wire rack and let cool completely. Store them at room temperature in an airtight container, where they will keep for a month or longer.

Yield: about 3 dozen biscotti

⋄ CRANBERRY PISTACHIO BISCOTTI ⋄

I worked out this recipe after I bought a package of Biscotti Nucci in a local market. The biscotti were delicious and the combination of pistachios and dried cranberries was a very happy one and particularly suitable for Christmas. My biscotti, while not an exact duplicate, are very pleasing and quite popular among my friends.

3 cups unbleached all-purpose flour	1 cup granulated sugar
2½ teaspoons baking powder	3 large eggs
½ teaspoon baking soda	Grated zest of 1 orange
½ teaspoon salt	½ teaspoon orange oil*
1 stick (¼ pound) unsalted butter, at room temperature	1 cup shelled pistachios
	1 cup dried cranberries

1. Preheat oven to 325°F. Line 2 cookie sheets with parchment paper.

2. In a medium-size bowl, whisk together the flour, baking powder, baking soda, and salt.

3. In the bowl of an electric mixer, beat the butter and sugar at medium speed until light and fluffy. Beat in the eggs, one at a time, then beat in the orange zest and orange oil.

---

*Boyajian, Inc., of Newton, Massachusetts, is the purveyor of excellent citrus oils—orange, lemon, and lime. They are superb products, completely natural, each essence squeezed from the rind of the fresh fruit. They are available by mail from The King Arthur Flour Baker's Catalogue (see page 117).

4. With mixer on low speed, gradually stir in the flour mixture until smooth, then stir in the pistachios and cranberries.

5. Divide the dough into thirds. Butter your fingers and shape each piece of dough into a log about 12 inches long and 2 inches in diameter. Place two of the logs 4 inches apart on one of the prepared cookie sheets and the third log on the other.

6. Bake for 30 minutes, until the logs turn a light golden color and are firm to the touch. Remove from the oven and reduce oven heat to 275°F. Place cookie sheets on wire racks and loosen logs with a metal spatula. Let them cool for 10 minutes.

7. Slide the baked logs onto a cutting board. With a long serrated knife, cut each log diagonally into ½-inch slices. Arrange the biscotti, cut side down, on the cookie sheets. Bake for an additional 40 minutes, turning the biscotti over once, until dry and toasted to a light golden color. Remove the biscotti to a wire rack and let cool completely. Store them at room temperature in an airtight container, where they will keep for up to a month.

Yield: 3½ to 4 dozen biscotti

• HAZELNUT ANISE BISCOTTI •

The combination of hazelnuts and anise make for very aromatic and crunchy biscotti. Make them part of a selection of two or three of the other biscotti in this section for a much-appreciated Christmas gift.

2 cups unbleached all-purpose flour
1 cup granulated sugar
1 teaspoon baking soda
Pinch of salt

3 large eggs, at room temperature
2 teaspoons anise extract
1 cup hazelnuts, toasted and skinned

1. Preheat oven to 350°F. Line 2 baking sheets with parchment paper.

2. In the bowl of an electric mixer, mix the flour, sugar, baking soda, and salt with the paddle.

3. In a small bowl, lightly beat the eggs and anise extract. Add the egg mixture to the dry ingredients and mix with the paddle at low speed until the dough just starts to come together. Stir in the hazelnuts and remove to a lightly floured surface.

4. Knead the dough lightly for a few minutes, then cover with a towel and let it rest for a few minutes. Divide the dough into thirds and shape each piece of dough into a 12-inch log about 2 inches in diameter. Place two of the logs 4 inches apart on one of the prepared cookie sheets and the third log on the other.

5. Bake for 30 minutes, until the logs turn a light golden color and are firm to the touch. Remove from the oven (leave the oven on) and place cookie sheets on wire racks. Loosen logs with a metal spatula and let them cool for 10 minutes.

6. Slide the baked logs onto a cutting board. With a long serrated knife, cut each log diagonally into ½-inch slices. Arrange the biscotti, cut side down, on the cookie sheets. Bake 12 to 15 minutes, turning the biscotti over once, until dry and toasted to a light golden color. Remove the biscotti to a wire rack and let cool completely. Store them at room temperature in an airtight container, where they will keep for up to a month.

Yield: about 3 dozen

• PEAR AND BLACK PEPPER BISCOTTI •

These unusual biscotti can be served either before a meal with an apéritif or at the end of a meal with a sweet dessert wine. For a special gift, combine the biscotti with some cheese and wine in a basket.

2 cups unbleached all-purpose flour
2 teaspoons coarsely ground black
   pepper
1 teaspoon baking powder
½ teaspoon baking soda
½ teaspoon salt
½ stick (4 tablespoons) unsalted
   butter, at room temperature

¼ cup granulated sugar
2 large eggs, at room temperature
2 large egg whites, at room
   temperature
1 cup finely chopped dried pears

1. Preheat oven to 350°F. Line a baking sheet with parchment paper.

2. In a medium-size bowl, whisk together the flour, black pepper, baking powder, baking soda, and salt.

3. In the bowl of an electric mixer, beat the butter and sugar at medium speed until light and fluffy. Beat in the eggs and egg whites, one at a time, to blend.

4. With the mixer on low speed, gradually beat in the flour mixture until well blended, then stir in the dried pears.

5. On a lightly floured surface, shape the dough into two logs 12 to 14 inches long and 2 inches in diameter. Place the logs 4 inches apart on the cookie sheet, and flatten them slightly with the palm of your hand. Bake for

20 to 25 minutes, until the logs are firm to the touch. Remove from the oven (leave the oven on) and place cookie sheets on wire racks. Loosen logs with a metal spatula and let them cool for 10 minutes.

6. Slide the baked logs onto a cutting board. With a long serrated knife, cut each log diagonally into ½-inch slices. Arrange the biscotti, cut side down, on the cookie sheets. Bake 12 to 15 minutes, turning the biscotti over once, until dry and toasted to a light golden color. Remove the biscotti to a wire rack and let cool completely. Store them at room temperature in an airtight container, where they will keep for up to a month.

Yield: about 3 dozen biscotti

> To receive a present handsomely and in a right spirit, even when you have none to give in return, is to give one in return.
> —Leigh Hunt

· RAISIN WALNUT RUSKS ·

I hesitate to call these cookies by the Italian *biscotti*, because this recipe comes from a Russian cookbook that was used by my grandmother, who worked as a professional chef for most of her life in Russia. We called them *sukhariki* (little toasts or rusks) and served them with tea, into which they are dunked. A strong, aromatic Earl Grey is the perfect tea to dunk these in.

1½ cups golden raisins
¼ cup Cognac
3 cups unbleached all-purpose flour
2½ teaspoons baking powder
½ teaspoon baking soda
½ teaspoon salt

1 stick (¼ pound) unsalted butter
½ cup granulated sugar
3 large eggs
½ teaspoon vanilla extract
¾ cup chopped walnuts

1. Macerate ¾ cup of the raisins in the Cognac for at least 1 hour.

2. Preheat oven to 325°F. Line a cookie sheet with parchment paper.

3. Place the remaining raisins, together with ½ cup of the flour, in the bowl of a food processor and pulse until the raisins are coarsely ground.

4. In a large bowl, whisk together the raisin-flour mixture, the remaining flour, baking powder, and salt.

5. In the bowl of an electric mixer, beat the butter and sugar at medium speed until light and fluffy. Beat in the eggs, one at a time, to blend. Drain the macerating raisins and stir them in, together with 1 teaspoon of the Cognac and the vanilla extract.

6. With mixer on low speed, gradually stir in the flour mixture until smooth, then stir in the walnuts by hand.

7. Divide the dough in half. Butter your fingers and shape each piece of dough into a log about 12 inches long and 2 inches in diameter. Place the logs 4 inches apart on the prepared cookie sheet.

8. Bake for 30 minutes, until the logs turn a light golden color and are firm to the touch. Remove from the oven and reduce oven heat to 250°F. Place cookie sheets on wire racks and loosen logs with a metal spatula. Let them cool for 10 minutes.

9. Slide the baked logs onto a cutting board. With a long serrated knife, cut each log diagonally into ½-inch slices. Arrange the biscotti, cut side down, on the cookie sheet. Bake for 30 minutes, turn the biscotti over, and bake for 30 minutes longer, until dry and toasted to a light golden color. Remove the biscotti to a wire rack and let cool completely. Store them at room temperature in an airtight container, where they will keep for up to a month.

Yield: 3½ to 4 dozen biscotti

• CHOCOLATE-DIPPED MOCHA BISCOTTI •

Delicious chocolate- and coffee-flavored biscotti are even more seductive when they are dipped in bittersweet chocolate.

2 cups unbleached all-purpose flour
1 cup sugar
2 tablespoons unsweetened cocoa
   powder
1 tablespoon instant coffee powder
1 teaspoon baking powder
½ teaspoon baking soda

¼ teaspoon salt
3 large eggs
1 teaspoon vanilla extract
2 ounces unsweetened chocolate,
   melted and cooled
For the chocolate dip:
6 ounces semisweet chocolate

1. Preheat oven to 325°F. Line a cookie sheet with parchment paper.

2. In a large bowl, whisk together the flour, sugar, cocoa powder, coffee powder, baking powder, baking soda, and salt.

3. In a medium-size bowl, whisk together the eggs, vanilla extract, and melted chocolate. Stir into the dry ingredients and mix until just incorporated.

4. Divide the dough in half with a rubber spatula. Flour your hands and shape each piece of dough into a log 12 to 14 inches long and about 2 inches in diameter. The dough will be sticky and you may need to flour your hands again. Arrange the logs at least 4 inches apart on the prepared cookie sheet.

5. Bake for 25 to 30 minutes, until the logs are firm to the touch. Remove from the oven and reduce oven heat to 300°F. Place cookie sheets on wire racks and loosen logs with a metal spatula. Let them cool for 10 minutes.

6. Slide the baked logs onto a cutting board. With a long serrated knife,

cut each log diagonally into ½-inch slices. Arrange the biscotti, cut side down, on the cookie sheet. Bake for 20 minutes, turn the biscotti over, and bake for 20 minutes longer. Remove the biscotti to a wire rack and let cool completely.

7. While biscotti are cooling, prepare the dipping chocolate: Chop the chocolate into small pieces and place it in the top of a double boiler set over (but not touching) barely simmering water to melt. When almost melted, remove from heat and stir until completely melted. Line 2 baking sheets with wax paper or foil. Dip both ends of each cool biscotto into the melted chocolate and lay them on the lined cookie sheets to cool and harden. Store at room temperature in an airtight container, where they will keep for up to a month.

Yield: 3½ to 4 dozen biscotti

Tea Cakes and Coffee Breads

· LEMON TEA CAKE ·

"Divoon!" is what my friend Winnie calls this lovely lemon-scented cake, which is kept moist with a lemon juice and Madeira glaze. It will certainly lift any afternoon tea to new heights, but serve it as a wonderful dessert as well. Or bake it in a loaf pan and give it as a gift.

2 cups all-purpose flour
2 teaspoons baking powder
¼ teaspoon salt
2 sticks (½ pound) unsalted butter,
  softened
1 cup granulated sugar

Grated rind of 2 lemons
4 large eggs
For the glaze:
1 cup confectioners' sugar
½ cup fresh lemon juice
½ cup dry Madeira

1. Preheat oven to 350°F. Prepare a 9-inch round cake pan by spraying the inside with nonstick vegetable spray or coating with butter, then dusting with flour and knocking out the excess.

2. Combine the flour, baking powder, and salt in a bowl and stir with a wire whisk to blend.

3. In the bowl of an electric mixer, cream the butter at medium speed. Raise speed to high and gradually beat in the sugar and grated lemon rind. Continue beating until the mixture is light and fluffy. Beat in the eggs, one at a time, until completely incorporated.

4. Lightly stir in the dry ingredients until just blended. Pour into the prepared cake pan and bake 25 to 35 minutes, until a tester inserted in the center comes out clean. The top of the cake should be a nice golden color.

5. Cool the cake on a wire rack for a few minutes and prick it all over with a fork. Remove cake from pan.

6. Mix together the confectioners' sugar, lemon juice, and Madeira until very smooth and fluid. Pour and spread the glaze all over the top of the cake and allow the cake to stand for several hours or overnight before serving. The glaze will seep down into the cake and keep it moist. Well wrapped, the cake will keep at room temperature for 4 or 5 days.

Yield: 6 to 8 servings

The only real blind person at Christmastime is he who has not Christmas in his heart.

—Helen Keller

• BISHOP'S BREAD •

I don't know why this is called Bishop's Bread. It was sent to me from a friend in Canada whose family has always made it for Christmas giving.

2¾ cups unbleached all-purpose
    flour
3 teaspoons baking powder
½ teaspoon salt
1 stick (¼ pound) unsalted butter,
    softened
¾ cup granulated sugar

2 large eggs
1 teaspoon vanilla extract
1 cup milk
⅓ cup chopped walnuts
⅓ cup dried cherries
⅓ cup semisweet chocolate chips
⅓ cup golden raisins

1. Preheat oven to 350°F. Prepare an 8½ × 4½ × 2½-inch loaf pan by spraying the inside with nonstick vegetable spray or coating with butter, then dusting with flour and knocking out the excess.

2. Combine the flour, baking powder, and salt in a bowl and stir with a wire whisk to blend.

3. In the bowl of an electric mixer, cream the butter at medium speed. Raise speed to high and gradually beat in the sugar. Continue beating until the mixture is light and fluffy. Beat in the eggs, one at a time, then vanilla extract, until completely incorporated.

4. Stir in the flour mixture alternating with the milk until well combined, then stir in the walnuts, dried cherries, chocolate chips, and raisins.

5. Pour into the prepared loaf pan and bake for about 1 hour, until a tester inserted in the center of the loaf comes out clean. The top will be cracked lengthwise down the center and a nice golden brown.

6. Turn out onto a wire rack and cool completely. Wrap tightly in plastic wrap. Store at room temperature up to 3 days or freeze for longer periods.

Yield: 1 loaf

A very old tradition in Eastern Europe involves cutting the branch of a cherry tree in December and forcing it to bloom. If the blossoms open in time for Christmas, it is believed to be a sign of good luck and a harbinger of an early spring.

• COGNAC GINGERBREAD WITH DRIED PLUMS •

Luscious summer plums! There is hardly anyone who wouldn't enjoy some lovely ripe plums. Dried plums? Sounds intriguing and appealing. Why then do prunes have such a negative reputation in this country? At the mention of prunes, people purse their lips, shake their heads, think of sick rooms and embarrassing moments, and never once think of how elegant and delicious a prune. . . . excuse me—*dried plum*—can be. I can change your mind once and for all with this very refined gingerbread cake. It is a great cake for Christmas, both to give and to serve. I usually make two.

1 cup chopped pitted prunes
½ cup Cognac
Unsweetened cocoa powder for dusting the pan
3 cups all-purpose flour
2 teaspoons baking soda
2 teaspoons ground ginger
1 teaspoon ground cinnamon
½ teaspoon ground cloves
⅛ teaspoon cayenne

½ teaspoon salt
1 cup solid vegetable shortening, at room temperature
1½ cups packed light brown sugar
4 large eggs
1 cup unsulfured molasses
¾ cup strong, brewed Earl Grey tea
1 teaspoon vanilla extract
¼ cup chopped crystallized ginger
3 tablespoons granulated sugar

1. Soak the prunes in the Cognac for 30 minutes.

2. Preheat oven to 350°F. Spray the inside of a 10-inch springform pan with nonstick baking spray. Dust with cocoa powder, then invert the pan and knock out the loose powder.

3. Place the prunes and the Cognac in a small pan and cook, uncovered, over medium-high heat until all the liquid has evaporated. Remove from heat and set aside.

4. In a bowl, whisk together the flour, baking soda, ginger, cinnamon, cloves, cayenne, and salt.

5. In another bowl, cream the shortening with an electric mixer at medium speed. Gradually beat in the sugar and continue beating until the mixture is light and fluffy. Beat in the eggs, one at a time, and gradually add the molasses, beating until well combined. Finally beat in ½ cup of the tea, vanilla, and flour mixture until the batter is just combined.

6. Turn batter into the prepared pan and sprinkle the crystallized ginger over the top. Bake for 1 hour and 10 to 20 minutes, or until a tester comes out clean.

7. Combine the remaining ¼ cup tea with the granulated sugar in a small saucepan. Bring to a boil and simmer for 5 minutes, until the sugar has completely dissolved and the syrup has cooked down by about half. Spoon the hot glaze over the warm cake.

8. Cool on wire rack for at least 1 hour before removing gingerbread from the pan. This cake will keep well wrapped at room temperature for up to 2 weeks.

Yield: 1 cake

• ALMOND CHERRY CORNMEAL TEA CAKE •

This may be my favorite recipe in the book. Everyone who tries this cake looks up in wonder and wants to know what's in it. I once had a houseguest, a thin, elegant woman who watches her diet with the stern vigilance of an army general, who couldn't get to sleep until she had consumed an entire mini loaf of this cake. Sometimes I bake it in a regular 9-inch cake pan, other times I bake it in mini-loaf bread pans. These mini loaves make perfect gifts at any time of year.

1¼ cups all-purpose flour
¾ cup yellow cornmeal, preferably coarsely ground
1 teaspoon baking powder
Pinch of salt
1½ sticks (12 tablespoons) unsalted butter, at room temperature
½ cup almond paste

1½ cups sugar
6 large eggs, separated and at room temperature
1 teaspoon vanilla extract
1 cup heavy cream
1 cup dried cherries, soaked in ¼ cup kirsch
Confectioners' sugar for topping

1. Preheat oven to 350°F. Spray the inside of a 9-inch round cake pan with nonstick vegetable spray and line the bottom of the cake pan with a round of parchment paper.

2. Combine the flour, cornmeal, baking powder, and salt in a bowl and stir with a wire whisk to blend.

3. In another bowl, cream the butter and almond paste with an electric mixer at medium speed. Raise speed to high and gradually beat in 1¼ cups

of the sugar. Continue beating until the mixture is light and fluffy. Beat in the egg yolks and vanilla extract until completely incorporated.

4. Stir the dry ingredients and heavy cream into the butter and egg mixture and blend well. Drain the cherries and stir them in. Set aside.

5. Beat the egg whites with the remaining ¼ cup of sugar until soft peaks form. Gently fold the egg whites into the cake mixture.

6. Pour the cake mixture into the prepared pan and bake for about 30 minutes, until the cake is golden, firm to the touch, and has drawn slightly away from the sides of the pan. Cool on a rack for 20 minutes before removing it from the pan.

7. Dust the top with confectioners' sugar and serve. When wrapped, the cake will keep for several days at room temperature, or several months in the freezer. Wrap the cake before you have dusted it with confectioners' sugar.

Yield: 6 to 8 servings

◆ GRAPEFRUIT-SCENTED CHRISTMAS CAKE ◆

I love lemon cake and any cake scented with orange, but I had never come across a cake that was flavored with grapefruit. Every year I prepare vodka infused with grapefruit zest (recipe follows) for special gifts. One year, as I was peeling off the aromatic zest, the idea for this cake came to me. I think you'll agree that it's a winner. Give it as a gift or serve it any time of day to family and friends. By the way, if you feel that the word "grapefruit" is sort of plain for a festive cake, try the French *pamplemousse*.

1½ cups unbleached all-purpose flour
1½ cups cake flour
½ teaspoon baking soda
½ teaspoon salt
2 sticks (½ pound) unsalted butter, at room temperature
4 tablespoons vegetable shortening
2½ cups superfine sugar

6 eggs, at room temperature
Zest of 1 large grapefruit, finely minced
1 tablespoon grapefruit-flavored vodka* (optional)
1 cup plain sour cream
¼ cup milk
For glaze:
¼ cup freshly squeezed grapefruit juice
¼ cup superfine sugar

---

*To make grapefruit-scented vodka: Add the zest of 1 grapefruit to 1 bottle of a good-quality Russian or Finnish vodka. The zest can be left in ribbons or finely minced. Let the vodka stand for 3 to 4 weeks before using it. Serve it ice cold from the freezer in tiny liqueur glasses, but not over ice.

1. Preheat oven to 325°F. Spray the inside of a 10-inch tube pan with nonstick vegetable spray, dust with flour, and tap out the excess.

2. In a medium-size bowl, whisk together the flours, baking soda, and salt.

3. In a large bowl, cream the butter and shortening with an electric mixer for 3 minutes at medium speed. Turn the speed to high and add the sugar gradually, until the mixture is very light and fluffy. Beat in the eggs, one at a time, blending well after each addition. Add all but 1 teaspoon of the grapefruit zest and the flavored vodka, if using. Reserve the remaining zest for the glaze.

4. With the mixer on low speed, add the dry ingredients alternately with the sour cream and finally the milk.

5. Pour the batter into the prepared pan and bake for about 1 hour and 20 minutes, until a tester inserted into the center comes out clean.

6. Cool the cake in the pan on a wire rack for 10 minutes, then invert the cake onto the rack and turn it right side up.

7. While the cake is cooling, mix the grapefruit juice with the sugar and the remaining 1 teaspoon grapefruit zest. Prick the top of the cake all over with a fork and spoon the glaze over the cake while it is still warm.

8. Let cool completely and store in an airtight container, where it will keep for up to 10 days. It will keep for several months in the freezer.

Yield: 1 cake, serving 12 to 16 people

· CARDAMOM PEAR CAKE ·

The combination of pears and cardamom is a heavenly one, and you will probably want to make several loaves of this fragrant, sweet, and spicy cake. It's a great gift and you will want to keep one for yourself to serve with tea, coffee, or a glass of wine.

1⅔ cups cake flour
4 teaspoons ground cardamom
1 teaspoon baking powder
¼ teaspoon salt
1½ sticks (12 tablespoons) unsalted butter, at room temperature

1 cup sugar
1 teaspoon grated lemon rind
3 eggs
⅓ cup whipping cream
1 cup finely diced dried pears

1. Preheat oven to 350°F. Prepare an 8½ × 4½ × 2½-inch loaf pan by spraying the inside with nonstick vegetable spray or coating with butter, then dusting with flour and knocking out the excess.

2. In a medium-size bowl, whisk together the flour, cardamom, baking powder, and salt.

3. In the bowl of an electric mixer, cream the butter at medium speed. Raise speed to high and gradually beat in the sugar and grated lemon rind. Continue beating until the mixture is light and fluffy. Beat in the eggs, one at a time, until completely incorporated. Turn speed to low, blend in the cream, and gradually stir in the flour mixture until thoroughly combined. Finally, fold in the diced pears by hand.

4. Pour the batter into the prepared pan and bake for 45 minutes, or until

a tester inserted into the center comes out clean. Remove pan from oven and allow to cool for 10 minutes before removing the cake from the pan to a wire rack. Cool completely, then wrap in plastic wrap. The cake will keep at room temperature for a few days and for several months in the freezer.

Yield: 10 to 12 slices

Is it not one of the mysteries of life that life should, after all, be so simple? Yes, as simple as Christmas, simple as this. Journeys through the dark to lighted door, arms open. Laughter-smothered kisses, kiss-smothered laughter. And blessedness in the heart of it all. Here are the verities, all made gay with tinsel! Dear, silly Christmas-card sayings and cracker mottoes—let them speak, let us sing! Dearer than memory, brighter than expectation is the ever returning *now* of Christmas. Why else, each time we greet its return, should happiness ring out in us like a peal of bells?

—Elizabeth Bowen

• CHOCOLATE CHIP BANANA LOAF •

The delicious but familiar banana bread gets a lift in this recipe by the addition of chocolate and coffee. The recipe is quick and easy and is a good one to remember when you are suddenly caught short and need to come up with some last-minute gifts. The original recipe was given to me by my friend, Robyn Low, and it is definitely one of the most popular gifts to come out of my kitchen.

1¾ cups unbleached all-purpose
   flour
2 teaspoons baking powder
½ teaspoon baking soda
½ teaspoon salt
1 stick (¼ pound) unsalted butter,
   at room temperature

⅔ cup granulated sugar
2 large eggs
1 cup mashed ripe banana (about 3
   bananas)
1 cup semisweet chocolate chips
1 tablespoon powdered instant coffee

1. Preheat oven to 375°F. Prepare a 9 × 5 × 3-inch loaf pan by spraying the inside with nonstick vegetable spray or coating with butter, then dusting with flour and knocking out the excess.

2. In a medium-size bowl, whisk together the flour, baking powder, baking soda, and salt. Set aside.

3. In the bowl of an electric mixer, cream the butter and the sugar until light and fluffy. Beat in the eggs, one at a time, until completely blended. Reduce speed to low and alternately stir the flour and the mashed bananas into the mixture.

4. With a spatula, fold in the chocolate chips and the instant coffee. Pour the mixture into the prepared loaf pan. Put it in the oven, reduce heat to 350°F, and bake for 45 to 60 minutes, until a tester inserted into the center of the loaf comes out clean.

5. Remove pan from oven and let cake cool in pan for 10 minutes before turning it out onto a rack to cool. Wrap tightly in plastic wrap and store at room temperature for up to 5 days or up to 3 months in the freezer.

Yield: 1 loaf

• HONEY SPICE BREAD •

The *pain d'épices* from France, *medivnyk* from the Ukraine, these are versions of gingerbread, sweetened with honey instead of molasses, and they appear in countries all over Europe and Eastern Europe. Many are made with rye flour alone. The history of this bread goes back all the way to the Middle Ages when Crusaders and spice merchants coming back from the Orient introduced many of the spices to European countries. The large amount of honey makes it a perfect keeping cake, because the honey acts as a preservative.

1 cup dark honey, such as
    buckwheat or avocado
¾ cup granulated sugar
Pinch of salt
2 teaspoons baking soda
1 teaspoon baking powder
¼ cup dark rum
1 teaspoon ground aniseed
1 teaspoon ground cinnamon
1 teaspoon ground ginger
½ teaspoon freshly grated nutmeg
¼ teaspoon ground cloves
2 cups rye flour
1½ cups unbleached all-purpose flour
1 cup chopped almonds
½ cup finely chopped golden raisins
¼ cup finely chopped candied lemon
    peel
1 tablespoon grated orange rind
1 tablespoon grated lemon rind

1. Preheat oven to 375°F. Butter two 7½ × 3½-inch loaf pans or four 5½ × 3 × 2⅛-inch pans and line them with wax paper on the bottom and both sides, with the paper extending on each side of the pan by a tab of about 2 inches.

2. Pour 1 cup hot water (120°F to 130°F) into a large mixing bowl. Add the honey, sugar, salt, baking soda, and baking powder and stir to dissolve.

3. Pour in the rum, aniseed, cinnamon, ginger, nutmeg, and cloves. Stir with a wooden spoon and continue stirring as you add 1 cup of the rye flour and 1 cup of the unbleached white flour. When completely mixed, stir in the remaining rye and white flours to make a thick batter. Stir in the almonds, raisins, candied peel, and grated orange and lemon rinds. Blend thoroughly and divide the dough among the prepared pans. They should be about three-quarters full.

4. Place the pans on the middle shelf in the oven. Bake for 10 minutes, reduce heat to 350°F, and continue baking for 50 minutes to 1 hour, until a wooden skewer inserted into the middle of a loaf comes out clean.

5. Remove the pans from the oven and place on wire cooling racks. Place pans on their sides and use the wax paper tabs to tug the loaves out of their pans. Let the breads cool completely and wrap tightly in plastic wrap, then in foil. Let the bread age at least 3 days before serving, or store the breads in a cool place for up to a month.

Yield: 2 loaves

We knew a woman who sold real estate in a small beach colony. She had a face like a brick wall, and a desire, some sixty years old and still undaunted, to play ingenue roles on Broadway. Her past was cautiously shaded.

We said we were going to live in France.

She said, "Where?"

We said, "Here, there—maybe Dijon . . ."

Suddenly her face was blasted. "Oh, Dijon!"

She put her hands up to her eyes and wept, and then cried fiercely: "The smell of it! The smell of Dijon gingerbread! When you are there smell it for me!"

So we did.

We smelled Dijon mustard, especially at the corner where Grey-Poupon flaunts little pots of it. We smelled Dijon cassis in the autumn, and stained our mouths with its metallic purple. But all year and everywhere we smelled the Dijon gingerbread, that *pain d'épice* which came perhaps from Asia with a tired Crusader.

—M.F.K. Fisher

Not-the-Usual
Fruitcakes

• VERY BERRY CHRISTMAS CAKE •

Have you tasted the many varieties of dried berries that are now available? Luscious dried strawberries? Intensely flavored wild blueberries? Lightly sweetened tart cranberries? Their concentrated flavors carry the essence of summer into the winter and make them a perfect ingredient for a Christmas fruitcake that no one will despise.

½ cup dried cranberries
½ cup dried blueberries
½ cup dried strawberries
½ cup dried cherries
½ cup golden raisins
½ cup light rum, plus additional
    rum for aging the cake
2 cups unbleached all-purpose flour

½ teaspoon baking powder
1 stick (¼ pound) unsalted butter,
    at room temperature
¾ cup granulated sugar
3 large eggs, lightly beaten
1 teaspoon vanilla extract
1 cup coarsely chopped pecans

1. The day before you bake the cake, combine all the dried berries and fruit in a bowl with the ½ cup rum. Cover and macerate until the following day.

2. Preheat oven to 350°F. Prepare two mini loaf (5½ × 3 × 2⅛-inch) pans or one 8½ × 4½ × 2¾-inch pan. Coat the inside with butter then line the bottom and sides with parchment paper.

3. In a medium-size bowl, whisk together the flour and baking powder and set aside.

4. In the bowl of an electric mixer, cream the butter until light and fluffy.

Gradually beat in the sugar and continue beating until well blended. Beat in the eggs, one at a time, and beat in the vanilla extract. Gradually beat in the flour, stir in the berries and their liquid, and stir in the nuts. Spoon the batter into the prepared pans.

5. Bake for 45 minutes to 1 hour, until a wooden skewer inserted into the center comes out clean. Remove the pans from the oven and let cake cool in pans for 10 minutes before turning them out onto wire racks. Peel off the parchment paper and let the cakes cool completely. Pierce the cake all over with a wooden skewer and spoon 1 to 2 tablespoons of rum over the cake. Moisten a double layer of cheesecloth with rum and wrap it around the cake. Wrap tightly in plastic wrap or in a heavy-duty plastic storage bag. Store the cakes in a cool spot (50°F to 60°F) or in the refrigerator. Check the cakes every two weeks to see if they are too dry. Unwrap them and brush on more rum to keep them from drying out. Store at room temperature for about 1 month and for at least 2 months in the refrigerator before serving.

Yield: 1 large or 2 small fruitcakes

> It is always so pleasant to be generous, though very vexatious to pay the debts.
>
> —Ralph Waldo Emerson

• CHOCOLATE FRUITCAKE •

A fruitcake with chocolate in it might be just the thing to change long-held opinions about fruitcakes. Here figs, apricots, cherries, and raisins are combined with chocolate for an elegant and sophisticated cake that tastes all the better when it has aged for several weeks.

½ cup chopped dried figs
½ cup chopped dried apricots
½ cup dried cherries
½ cup golden raisins
¼ cup Grand Marnier
¼ cup Cognac, plus additional
  Cognac for aging the cake

½ cup unbleached all-purpose flour
½ teaspoon baking powder
3 ounces unsweetened chocolate
1 stick (¼ pound) unsalted butter,
  at room temperature
1 cup granulated sugar
3 large eggs, at room temperature

1. In a small bowl, combine the figs, apricots, cherries, and raisins with the Grand Marnier and ¼ cup Cognac. Cover and let the fruit macerate for 24 hours, stirring it occasionally.

2. Preheat oven to 325°F. Prepare three mini loaf (5⅓ × 2⅛-inch) pans or one 9 × 5 × 3-inch pan. Coat the insides with butter then line the bottom and sides with parchment paper.

3. In a small bowl, whisk together the flour and baking powder.

4. Melt the chocolate in the top of a double boiler set over (but not touching) barely simmering water. When almost melted, remove from heat and stir until completely melted. Set aside.

5. In the bowl of an electric mixer, beat the butter and sugar together

until light and fluffy. Beat in the melted chocolate until completely blended. Scrape down the sides of the bowl, then beat in the eggs, one at a time, until completely blended. Scrape down the sides of the bowl with a rubber spatula as needed. With the mixer on low speed, blend in the flour, then the fruit and liquor.

6. Spoon the batter into the prepared pans and bake for an hour to an hour and 15 minutes, until a wooden skewer inserted into the center comes out just slightly moist. Remove pans from oven and let cakes cool in pans.

7. Peel off the parchment paper and brush the cakes all over with Cognac. Moisten a double layer of cheesecloth with Cognac and wrap it around the cakes. Wrap tightly in plastic wrap or in a heavy-duty plastic storage bag. Store the cakes in a cool spot (50°F to 60°F) or in the refrigerator. Check the cakes every week or so to see if the cheesecloth has dried, and brush on more Cognac to keep them from drying out. Store at cool temperature for about 1 month and for at least 2 months in the refrigerator before serving.

Yield: 1 large or 3 small fruitcakes

• FIGGY ALMOND CHRISTMAS CAKE •

This uncomplicated cake features figs and almonds, keeps very well despite its lack of alcohol, and is eminently suitable for Christmas giving. It is much appreciated by those who shy away from fruitcakes with too many ingredients in them.

1½ cups stemmed and chopped
   dried figs
½ cup orange juice
½ cup ground almonds
1½ cups unbleached all-purpose
   flour
1 teaspoon baking powder
1½ sticks (12 tablespoons) unsalted
   butter, at room temperature

¾ cup granulated sugar
3 large eggs, lightly beaten
Grated zest of 1 orange
½ cup sliced almonds
For finishing the cake:
½ cup orange or lemon juice
½ cup granulated sugar

1. In a small bowl, combine the figs and the orange juice and set aside.

2. Preheat oven to 350°F. Butter an 8-cup kugelhopf mold and sprinkle with the ground almonds.

3. In a small mixing bowl, whisk together the flour and baking powder.

4. In the bowl of an electric mixer, cream the butter and sugar until light and fluffy. Beat in the eggs, one at a time, and continue beating until the mixture becomes very pale. Beat in the orange zest. With mixer speed on low, gradually mix in the flour mixture until just blended. Finally, stir in the figs and orange juice and the sliced almonds.

5. Turn the batter into the prepared pan and bake for 40 to 45 minutes, until a wooden skewer inserted into the center comes out clean. Remove pan from oven and let cake cool in the pan for 10 minutes. Remove cake to a wire rack to cool completely.

6. In a small saucepan, bring the orange juice and sugar to a boil over medium heat. Remove from heat and stir with a wooden spoon until the sugar is completely dissolved. Pierce the top of the cake all over with a wooden skewer and spoon the warm syrup over the cake. When the cake has absorbed the liquid, wrap in plastic and foil, then store in a cool place for up to 2 weeks or freeze for up to 3 months.

Yield: 1 cake

I heard the bells on Christmas Day
Their old, familiar carols play,
And wild and sweet
The words repeat
Of peace on earth, good-will to men!
—Henry Wadsworth Longfellow

• IRISH GUINNESS FRUITCAKE •

I was intrigued when I came across this fruitcake recipe in Jane Grigson's *British Cookery* (New York: Atheneum, 1985). As more and more flavorful beer becomes available in this country, the possibilities for using it as an ingredient multiply. In this case, the dark, rich flavor of Guinness beer provides a perfect backdrop to the sweet, spicy flavors of the traditional fruitcake.

1 cup dark raisins
½ cup golden raisins
2 cups Guinness stout or porter
1¼ cups unbleached all-purpose flour
1 cup cake flour
1 teaspoon baking powder
½ teaspoon salt
½ teaspoon ground cinnamon

½ teaspoon freshly grated nutmeg
½ teaspoon ground cloves
1 stick (¼ pound) unsalted butter, at room temperature
1 cup tightly packed dark brown sugar
3 large eggs, lightly beaten
Grated rind of 1 orange
½ cup chopped walnuts

1. Soak the raisins in the stout or porter for 12 to 24 hours.

2. Preheat oven to 325°F. Butter the insides of an 8-inch round cake pan, line the bottom with a round of parchment paper, and butter the parchment paper.

3. In a medium-size bowl, whisk together the flours, baking powder, salt, cinnamon, nutmeg, and cloves.

4. In the bowl of an electric mixer, cream the butter and sugar until light

and fluffy. Add the eggs, one at a time, beating until each is well blended. With the mixer on low speed, gradually stir in the flour mixture and orange rind. Drain the raisins, reserving the beer, and fold in the raisins and walnuts.

5. Turn the batter into the prepared cake pan and bake for 1 hour. Turn oven heat down to 300°F and bake for 1 to 1½ hours longer, until a wooden skewer inserted into the center comes out clean. Remove cake from oven and place it on a wire rack to cool in its pan.

6. When the cake has cooled, turn it out of the pan, peel away the parchment paper, and pierce holes all around the bottom of the cake with a skewer. Pour 1 cup of the reserved beer into the pierced cake. Soak a double layer of cheesecloth in beer and wrap it around the cake. Store it in a plastic container with a tight-fitting lid in a cool place for 2 weeks before using. Freeze it for up to 2 months.

Yield: 1 cake

I was eighteen when I first tasted a Christmas fruitcake, which may explain why I liked it so much. My family never celebrated Christmas, except by watching the first fifteen minutes of "Amahl and the Night Visitors" on television, and nothing in my grandmothers' repertory had prepared me for that first wondrous mouthful at the house of a friend from college.

—Jeffrey Steingarten

Festive Yeast Breads

• CHRISTMAS WREATH BREAD •

This spectacular bread shaped into a large wreath tastes as good as it looks. The inside is a mellow golden color from the saffron and the raisins, and the hint of almonds in the sweet dough make this bread especially delicious. Serve it for breakfast or brunch on Christmas day.

½ teaspoon saffron threads
½ cup boiling water
2 packages active dry yeast
3 large eggs, at room temperature
½ cup granulated sugar
¼ teaspoon salt
½ cup sour cream, at room temperature
¼ cup ground almonds
1 teaspoon vanilla extract
½ teaspoon almond extract
1 teaspoon grated lemon zest

1 stick (¼ pound) unsalted butter, at room temperature
3½ to 4 cups unbleached all-purpose flour
½ cup golden raisins
Glaze and topping:
1 egg, beaten with 1 teaspoon heavy cream or milk
Icing:
½ cup confectioners' sugar
2 teaspoons fresh lemon juice
½ teaspoon almond extract

1. In the bowl of heavy-duty mixer fitted with a paddle, steep the saffron threads in the boiling water and let stand to cool a little. When the water feels warm but not hot, sprinkle in the yeast and stir to dissolve. Beat in the eggs, one at a time, followed by the sugar, salt, sour cream, ground almonds, vanilla extract, almond extract, and lemon zest. Finally, beat in tablespoonfuls of butter alternating with half cups of flour until you have added all the

butter and the mixture forms a dough that starts to come away from the sides of the bowl.

2. Remove the dough to a lightly floured surface and let it rest while you wash and butter the bowl. Knead the dough gently, adding any remaining flour to make a smooth but relatively soft dough. Place the dough in the buttered bowl, cover loosely with a kitchen towel, and let rise in a warm place until doubled, about 2 hours.

3. Line a baking sheet with parchment paper. Remove the dough once more to a lightly floured surface. Pinch off a piece of dough the size of a golf ball and reserve. Pat out the remaining dough, spread the raisins over the surface, and knead gently to incorporate them into the dough. Divide the dough in half and roll each piece of dough into a log about 24 inches long. Twist the two logs together and form into a circle on the prepared baking sheet, pinching the ends together. Roll the reserved piece of dough into a long, thin strand and make a bow with it. Paint the wreath all over with the egg glaze and place the bow over the area where the wreath is joined together. Paint the bow with the egg glaze. Let it rise for 30 minutes and paint it with the egg glaze again.

4. Preheat oven to 350°F.

5. Bake for 30 to 40 minutes, until a wooden skewer inserted into the center comes out clean. Remove from oven and cool on a wire rack.

6. This bread is best when it is served the same day it is baked, and best of all, when it is still warm. This is hard to do on a busy holiday like Christmas. It can be baked the day before and reheated in a 300°F oven for 15 to 20 minutes, and it is best to apply the icing after it is reheated. Or it can be wrapped well and frozen for up to 2 months, then thawed at room temperature and reheated and iced.

7. To make the icing, mix the confectioners' sugar, lemon juice, and almond extract in a small bowl. Apply the icing while the wreath is still warm. The best way to do it is with your fingers.

Yield: 1 large wreath

The Christmas wreath is a tradition that has its origins in pagan customs. But for Christians, the circular shape symbolizes God's eternal love, and its greenery signifies Christ's immortality.

• CHRISTMAS STOLLEN •

This is my interpretation of the famous Christmas bread from Germany. Once again, I have replaced candied fruits with a combination of dried apricots, raisins, and cherries. It is a delicious bread that keeps well and deserves a place at the Christmas breakfast table. It is particularly good when thinly sliced and toasted. A wonderfully generous Christmas gift.

1 cup coarsely chopped dried apricots
1 cup golden raisins
1 cup dried cherries
¼ cup dark rum
1 cup whole milk
1½ sticks (12 tablespoons) unsalted butter
1 teaspoon vanilla extract
2 packages active dry yeast

5 cups unbleached all-purpose flour
½ cup sugar
½ teaspoon salt
3 large eggs, lightly beaten
For the filling and topping:
6 tablespoons unsalted butter, melted
4 tablespoons granulated sugar
2 tablespoons confectioners' sugar
3 tablespoons dark rum

1. Combine the apricots, raisins, cherries, and rum in a bowl and mix them well. Let stand for at least 1 hour, or longer if you remember to do it (overnight is good).

2. In a small heavy saucepan, scald the milk and remove from heat. Cut up the butter and add it to the milk. Stir in the vanilla extract and keep stirring until the butter is melted.

3. In the bowl of a heavy-duty electric mixer fitted with a paddle, mix the yeast with 3 cups of the flour, the sugar, and salt. When the milk is no longer

hot but warm (130°F), make a well in the center of the flour and pour in the milk and the eggs. Beat the mixture until it is smooth. Mix in the rum-soaked fruit and let it rest for 15 minutes.

4. Switch to a dough hook or stir in the remaining flour with a wooden spoon. If using a dough hook, knead the dough for 5 minutes at low speed. Otherwise, turn the dough out onto a lightly floured surface and knead the dough until it feels satiny and resilient. Place the dough into a well-buttered bowl, cover loosely with a kitchen towel, and let rise in a warm place until doubled, 1 to 1½ hours.

5. Line a baking sheet with parchment paper. Punch down the dough and turn it out onto a lightly floured surface. Divide the dough in half and press each half into an oval, about 12 inches long and 8 inches at its widest point. Brush each oval with 1 tablespoon of the melted butter and sprinkle with 1 tablespoon of the granulated sugar. Fold each oval in half lengthwise and place on prepared baking sheet. Cover with a kitchen towel and let rise for about 30 minutes, until the dough has risen but not doubled.

6. Preheat oven to 350°F.

7. Brush each loaf with 1 tablespoon of melted butter and sprinkle with 1 tablespoon of the granulated sugar. Bake for 25 to 30 minutes, until a wooden skewer inserted into the center comes out clean. Remove from oven and brush each stollen with the remaining melted butter, sprinkle with 1 tablespoon confectioners' sugar, and drizzle with 1½ tablespoons dark rum. Remove the stollen to wire cooling racks. When the stollen are completely cooled, wrap them tightly in plastic wrap and foil. Stollen will keep at room temperature for up to 10 days and they can be frozen for up to 3 months.

Yield: 2 stollen

• CHOCOLATE-FLECKED KUGELHOPF •

Many years ago I found the original of this recipe in *Gourmet* magazine. It was sent in by a reader and was named in honor of her aunt, Sari Lengyel, who had given her the recipe. I've made it many times and made a number of changes to suit my taste, but the idea of incorporating chocolate into a kugelhopf comes from there, and it's a winner. Kugelhopf, as you may know, is a cross between a bread and a cake and you can serve it for breakfast, afternoon tea, or dessert. Naturally it makes a wonderful gift.

2 cups whole milk
2 sticks (½ pound) unsalted butter
¾ cup granulated sugar
1 teaspoon vanilla extract
½ teaspoon salt

5½ cups unbleached all-purpose flour
2 packages active dry yeast
3 large egg yolks
6 ounces semisweet chocolate, grated

1. In a medium-size saucepan, scald the milk and remove from heat. Stir in 1 stick of butter, ½ cup of the sugar, the vanilla extract, and salt. When the butter has melted, transfer the milk to the bowl of a heavy-duty electric mixer and let cool to lukewarm. Use the paddle attachment to stir in 2½ cups of the flour and the yeast at low speed. Stir in the egg yolks and the remaining 3 cups of flour, adding it ½ cup at a time to make a smooth dough.

2. Remove the dough to a lightly floured surface and knead briefly until the dough feels smooth and satiny. Wash, dry, and lightly butter the bowl and replace the dough. Let it rise in a warm place, covered loosely with a kitchen towel, for 1 hour, until doubled in bulk.

3. Melt the remaining stick of butter and let it cool. Butter the inside of a kugelhopf mold or angel food pan and dust with flour, knocking out the excess.

4. When the dough has risen, punch it down and remove it to a lightly floured surface. Pat the dough into a rectangle and work the chocolate into the dough by folding it up and spreading it out again, adding more chocolate each time, until all the chocolate is worked in. Pat the dough into a large rectangle (about 15 × 10 inches). Spread the melted butter over the dough and sprinkle with the remaining ¼ cup sugar. Roll up the dough, starting with the long side, and arrange it in the prepared pan, pinching the ends together. Cover loosely with a kitchen towel and let it stand in a warm place until the dough reaches the top of the pan, about 1 hour.

5. Preheat oven to 350°F.

6. Bake the kugelhopf for 45 minutes to 1 hour, until a wooden skewer inserted into the center comes out clean. Remove from oven and turn out of the pan onto a wire rack. Let cool completely. If you are not serving it the same day, wrap well in plastic wrap or foil and freeze for up to 3 months. Dust with confectioners' sugar before serving.

Yield: 1 kugelhopf

• PANETTONE •

There are many wonderful versions of this Italian Christmas bread, and this one, with its abundance of raisins, is one of my favorites. The amount of sugar is more than is usually called for, and if you wish you can reduce it to as little as ¼ cup. Traditionally these breads are baked in tall, straight-sided pans especially made for panettone, but they are not absolutely necessary.

1 cup golden raisins
2 tablespoons Grand Marnier or
    dark rum
4½ cups unbleached all-purpose
    flour
¾ cup granulated sugar
2 packages active dry yeast
½ teaspoon salt

½ cup pine nuts
1 teaspoon grated lemon zest
1 cup whole milk
1 stick (¼ pound) unsalted butter
3 large eggs, lightly beaten
For the icing:
1 cup confectioners' sugar
4 tablespoons heavy cream

1. In a small bowl, combine the raisins and Grand Marnier.

2. In the bowl of a heavy-duty electric mixer fitted with a paddle, combine 3 cups of the flour, sugar, yeast, salt, pine nuts, and lemon zest.

3. In a medium-size saucepan, scald the milk over medium-high heat. Remove from the heat, add the butter, and let it stand until the butter has melted and the milk is no longer hot but warm (about 130°F).

4. Make a well in the center of the flour mixture and pour in the milk mixture and the eggs. Starting at low speed, beat the mixture until it is well combined and smooth. Stir in the raisins and their liquid, and gradually stir

in the remaining flour. Cover loosely with a towel and let rise in a warm place until doubled, about 1 hour.

5. While the dough is rising, prepare the pans. You will need either two 2-pound coffee cans or two 9-inch springform pans. Butter the insides of the cans or pans generously. If you are using coffee cans, cut out 2 rounds of parchment paper and put one on the bottom of each can. If you are using springform pans, you will need to make a collar for each pan. Cut two 27-inch lengths of parchment paper and fold each piece in half lengthwise. Fit each length of parchment paper inside the springform pan so that the ends overlap, then secure them with a paper clip.

6. Punch down the dough to remove any air bubbles, then divide the dough in half. Press the dough into the prepared cans or pans, pressing it in gently with your fingers. Cover and let rise for 45 minutes to 1 hour, until doubled.

7. Preheat oven to 350°F.

8. Bake for 40 to 45 minutes, until a wooden skewer inserted into the center comes out clean. Remove from oven and turn out of the cans or pans and cool on wire racks. Wrapped tightly, these will keep at room temperature for 4 or 5 days and up to 2 months in the freezer. Freeze them without the icing.

9. Just before serving, mix together the confectioners' sugar and cream and brush tops of the panettone with this icing.

Yield: 2 panettone loaves

• *MAKOWNIK*: POLISH POPPY SEED BREAD •

I am passionate about poppy seeds. Many years ago, when I was just out of college and had my first apartment in Manhattan, there was a Viennese bakery and café on Third Avenue in the upper seventies where they made a poppy seed strudel that was out of this world. I would stop in every Saturday afternoon for tea and strudel and often a whole strudel would come home with me to sustain me during the week. When it closed years later because the landlord sold the building and it was going to be torn down, it was my first inkling that life did not always change for the better. When I make this poppy seed bread at Christmastime it reminds me of those days when I was young and there was poppy seed strudel just around the corner. This is a traditional Christmas bread in many parts of Eastern Europe and especially Poland. The recipe comes to me from my friend, Helena Goscilo, whose family always had it at Christmas.

For the dough:
2 packages active dry yeast
¼ cup warm water
1 cup whole milk
¾ cup granulated sugar
½ teaspoon salt
1 stick plus 2 tablespoons unsalted
   butter

2 teaspoons vanilla extract
1 large egg plus 2 large egg yolks,
   lightly beaten
4 to 5 cups unbleached all-purpose
   flour

For the filling:
½ stick (4 tablespoons) unsalted
  butter
1 pound ground poppy seeds★
1 cup whole milk
1 cup granulated sugar

½ cup golden raisins
¼ cup ground almonds
Grated zest of 1 lemon
3 tablespoons honey
2 large egg whites

For the glaze:
1 large egg, lightly beaten

1. In the bowl of a heavy-duty electric mixer fitted with a paddle, dissolve the yeast in the warm water, with a pinch of sugar and a pinch of flour.

2. In a small heavy saucepan, bring the milk, sugar, and salt just to the boil and remove from heat. Cut the butter into pieces and stir it into the milk. Stir in the vanilla extract. Let it cool down to very warm (130°F) but not hot.

3. Add the milk mixture and the eggs to the yeast and stir to blend. With the mixer on low, add the flour ½ cup at a time. When the mixture starts to become quite thick, switch to a dough hook or remove the dough to a lightly floured surface. Knead the dough about 4 minutes, incorporating as much of the remaining flour as needed to make a soft but slightly sticky dough. Wash, dry, and butter the mixing bowl. Gather the dough into a ball, put it in the bowl, and turn it to coat with the butter. Cover loosely with a

---

★Available from: Paprikas Weiss, 1572 Second Avenue, New York, N.Y. 10028, (212) 288-6117.

kitchen towel and let rise in a warm place until doubled in bulk, 1 to 1½ hours.

4. Prepare the filling: In a medium-size saucepan, melt the butter over medium heat. Add the poppy seeds, milk, sugar, raisins, almonds, lemon zest, and honey and cook the mixture, stirring constantly, until it becomes thick enough to spread, 10 to 15 minutes, then remove from heat. Beat the egg whites with an electric mixer until they hold soft peaks, then fold them into the poppy seed mixture.

5. Line a baking sheet with parchment paper. Turn the dough out onto a lightly floured surface and roll it out into a large rectangle (about 12 × 10 inches). Spread the poppy seed filling over the surface, leaving a ¾-inch border all around. Staring with the longer side, roll up the dough, jelly roll fashion, and transfer it seam side down onto the prepared baking sheet. Cover the dough with a kitchen towel and let rise until puffy, but not double, about 1 hour.

6. Preheat oven to 375°F.

7. Brush the risen loaf with the egg and bake for 50 minutes to 1 hour, until a wooden skewer inserted into the center comes out clean. Remove from oven and transfer the bread to a wire rack to cool. Although the bread is best when eaten within 1 or 2 days, it will keep, tightly wrapped, at room temperature for up to 5 days. It will keep frozen for up to 3 months.

Yield: 1 poppy seed bread

Savory Treats

• GOMASIO BREADSTICKS •

Crunchy, salty, and full of rich sesame flavor from the gomasio seasoning, these breadsticks make a wonderful gift for the person who likes to nibble on something but doesn't care for sweets. Or make them for yourself and serve them with drinks or as an accompaniment to a simple soup supper.

You can buy prepared gomasio in any health food store, but it always tastes better and fresher if you make it yourself.

3 cups unbleached all-purpose flour
2 tablespoons gomasio (recipe follows)
1 tablespoon granulated sugar
2 packages active dry yeast
1¼ cups warm water (about 130°F)

¼ cup extra-virgin olive oil, plus additional olive oil for coating the sticks
1 large egg white, beaten with 1 tablespoon water
Sesame seeds for topping
Kosher salt for topping

1. Place the flour, gomasio, sugar, and yeast in the bowl of a food processor outfitted with the steel blade. Pulse on and off to combine. With the processor on, pour in the water and olive oil through the feeding tube. Process until well combined into a smooth dough.

2. Remove the dough to a lightly floured surface and shape it into a log about 20 inches long. Cut the log into 1-inch pieces. Roll each piece of dough into a rope that is as long as your baking sheet. Line 2 baking sheets with parchment paper. Coat your palms with olive oil and spread the oil over each stick. Arrange side by side, about 1 inch apart on the baking sheets, and let rise for about 15 minutes, until the sticks are a little puffy.

3. Preheat oven to 300°F.

4. Use a pastry brush to coat each stick with the egg white, then sprinkle with sesame seeds and salt. Bake the breadsticks for 40 to 50 minutes, switching the pans around halfway through the baking time, until they are a golden brown color. Cool on wire racks and store in an airtight container for up to 2 weeks.

Yield: 20 breadsticks

• GOMASIO •

Gomasio (a Japanese word) is a wonderful seasoning salt with the rich, full flavor of toasted sesame seeds. Use it instead of table salt to enhance steamed vegetables, salads, or any other food to which you might want to add salt. A jar of gomasio makes an original and welcome stocking stuffer.

1 cup unhulled sesame seeds   *4 teaspoons sea salt, or to taste*

1. Rinse the seeds in several changes of cold water and drain well.
2. Place a heavy cast-iron skillet over medium-high heat and put in the sesame seeds. Roast the seeds, stirring constantly, for 8 to 12 minutes, until they have started to color and give off a pleasant, toasted aroma. Add the salt for the last minute of roasting.
3. Transfer the sesame seeds and salt to a food processor and pulse on and off a few times to a coarse ground consistency. Taste and add more salt if you wish. Cool completely and store (indefinitely) in the refrigerator in a tightly covered jar.

Yield: 1 cup gomasio

· LEMON PARMESAN CRISPS ·

I love these spicy, lemony, cheesy crisps and find them addictive at the cocktail hour, or any other hour I can get my hands on them. Pack them in a pretty tin and pair it with a good bottle of dry sherry for a thoughtful gift.

1½ cups (about ¼ pound) freshly grated imported Parmesan
¾ cup unbleached all-purpose flour
1 teaspoon freshly grated lemon zest
½ teaspoon coarsely ground black pepper

¼ teaspoon cayenne, or more to taste
½ stick (4 tablespoons) unsalted cold butter
1 tablespoon water
2 teaspoons fresh lemon juice

1. Place the Parmesan, flour, lemon zest, black pepper, and cayenne in the bowl of a food processor outfitted with the steel blade. Pulse on and off to combine.

2. Cut the butter into small bits and add it to the cheese-and-flour mixture. Pulse on and off until the mixture resembles coarse meal. Sprinkle on the water and lemon juice and pulse until it just starts to form a dough. Remove to a lightly floured surface and knead briefly until the dough holds together. Place the dough on a sheet of plastic wrap and form it into a log about 11 inches long and 1½ inches wide. Wrap it tightly in the plastic wrap and refrigerate for at least 1 hour, until it is firm enough to slice. (The dough will keep in the refrigerator for 2 or 3 days, or for a month in the freezer.)

3. Preheat oven to 375°F. Line 2 baking sheets with parchment paper.

4. Cut the log into ¼-inch slices and arrange them 1 inch apart on the

baking sheets. Bake them one sheet at a time for about 10 minutes, or until they are golden around the edges. Use a metal spatula to move the baked crisps to wire cooling racks and let them cool completely. Store in an airtight container for up to 2 weeks.

Yield: 3½ dozen crisps

> My best of wishes for your Merry Christmases, and your happy New Years, your long lives and your true prosperities.
> —Charles Dickens

• SPICY CHEESE CRISPS •

There are many variations of this delicious spicy cookie and this one is my current favorite. These cookies are at their best when served warm, so you should freeze them after they are baked and warm them briefly before serving. I can't think of a nicer gift, only be sure to include a card with warming instructions.

1¾ cups unbleached all-purpose
   flour
½ teaspoon salt
½ teaspoon dry mustard
¼ teaspoon cayenne
¼ teaspoon ground white pepper

1½ sticks (12 tablespoons) unsalted
   butter, at room temperature
½ cup shredded sharp Cheddar cheese
2 large egg yolks
1 teaspoon Worcestershire sauce

1. In a medium-size bowl, whisk together the flour, salt, mustard, cayenne, and white pepper.

2. In the bowl of an electric mixer, cream together the butter and cheese until well blended. Beat in the egg yolks and Worcestershire sauce. On low speed, stir in the flour mixture to make a smooth dough. Divide the dough in half, wrap in plastic, and refrigerate for 1 hour.

3. Preheat oven to 350°F. Line 2 baking sheets with parchment paper.

4. On a lightly floured surface, roll out one portion of dough at a time to a ¼-inch thickness. Using a 2-inch fluted cookie cutter, cut out rounds and arrange them on the prepared baking sheets.

5. Bake for 10 to 12 minutes, until the cookies turn golden brown. Serve

them directly from the oven or cool on wire racks for storing. Pack in layers between sheets of wax paper in an airtight container and freeze for up to 3 months. Place the cookies straight from the freezer into a preheated 300°F oven for about 10 minutes and serve.

Yield: about 4 dozen crisps

• CHEESY WALNUT BISCUITS •

I found the original of this recipe in a wonderful little book called *The English Biscuit and Cookie Book,* by Sonia Allison (New York: St. Martin's Press, 1983). I have made these biscuits many times, slowly changing the ingredients to suit my taste. They are great savory biscuits, equally good with a glass of wine or an afternoon cup of tea.

1¾ cups unbleached all-purpose
    flour
½ teaspoon salt
¼ teaspoon ground white pepper
1½ sticks (12 tablespoons) unsalted
    butter, refrigerator cold
½ cup finely shredded Gruyère
    cheese

⅓ cup finely chopped walnuts
1 large egg yolk
1 to 2 tablespoons cold water
Topping:
1 large egg white, beaten until foamy
¼ cup shredded Parmesan cheese
¼ cup finely chopped walnuts

1. Combine the flour, salt, and pepper in the bowl of a food processor fitted with a metal blade. Pulse several times to blend.

2. Cut the butter into small pieces and add to the flour mixture. Process until the mixture resembles coarse meal. Add the cheese and walnuts and process to blend. With the processor running, add the egg yolk and 1 table-spoon of water through the feed tube. Add more water, if necessary, to make a dough that just starts to hold together. Scoop out the dough, wrap in plastic, and refrigerate for 1 hour.

3. Preheat oven to 350°F. Line 2 baking sheets with parchment paper.

4. On a lightly floured surface, roll out the dough to a thickness of ¼ inch. Cut out rounds with a 2-inch fluted cookie cutter and place them on the prepared baking sheets. Brush the cookies with the egg white and sprinkle with Parmesan cheese and walnuts.

5. Bake for 15 to 20 minutes, until the biscuits turn a pale golden color. Transfer to wire racks and cool completely. Store the biscuits in an airtight container for up to 2 weeks, or freeze them for up to 3 months.

Yield: about 2½ dozen biscuits

• CORNMEAL SAGE BREADSTICKS •

You will love these crunchy, chewy breadsticks, made aromatic with fresh sage. If you must substitute dry sage, use only half the amount called for.

1¼ cups lukewarm water
1½ teaspoons active dry yeast (half a ¼-ounce package)
1 tablespoon malt syrup, or 1 teaspoon honey
¼ cup extra-virgin olive oil

1½ teaspoons salt
¾ cup yellow cornmeal, preferably stone-ground
3 cups unbleached all-purpose flour
¼ cup finely chopped fresh sage

1. In the bowl of a heavy-duty electric mixer fitted with a paddle, combine the water, yeast, and malt syrup. Stir briefly and let it stand for 10 minutes, until foamy. On low speed, stir in the olive oil, salt, and cornmeal. Stir in the flour, ½ cup at a time, until the dough starts to come together. Add the sage, switch to the dough hook, and knead at low speed for about 3 minutes. Remove the dough to a lightly floured surface and knead by hand for a few minutes, until you have a smooth, satiny dough. Form into a ball and place in a lightly oiled bowl. Cover with plastic and let rise for 1 hour, until doubled in size.

2. Remove dough to a lightly floured surface and shape it into a log about 20 inches long. Cut the log into 1-inch pieces. Roll each piece of dough into a rope that is as long as your baking sheet. Line 2 baking sheets with parchment paper. Coat your palms with olive oil and spread the oil over each stick. Arrange side by side, about 1 inch apart on the baking sheets, and let rise for about 15 minutes, until the sticks are a little puffy.

3. Preheat oven to 450°F. Bake the breadsticks for about 20 minutes, switching the pans around halfway through the baking time, until they are a golden brown color. Cool on wire racks and store in an airtight container for up to 2 weeks, or freeze for up to 3 months.

Yield: 20 breadsticks

It is in the giving that we receive . . .

—St. Francis of Assisi

Mail-Order Sources for Equipment and Supplies

Williams-Sonoma
Mail Order Department
P.O. Box 7456
San Francisco, California 94120-7456
(415) 421-4242
Special pans, cookie sheets, etc.

Maid of Scandinavia
32-44 Raleigh Avenue
Minneapolis, Minnestoa 55416
(800) 328-6722
Special pans, baking equipment, cookie cutters, decorating equipment, colored and crystal sugars

The Bridge Company
214 East 52nd Street
New York, New York 10022
(212) 688-4220
Special pans, molds, cookie cutters, etc.

The King Arthur Flour Baker's Catalogue
P.O. Box 876
Norwich, Vermont 05055
(800) 827-6836
Excellent variety of flours, many stone-ground and organic, as well as flavorings and spices, Boyajian citrus oils, parchment paper in sheets

Walnut Acres
Penns Creek, Pennsylvania 17862
(717) 837-3874
Large selection of flours and grains; very good selection of dried fruits (many organic) and nuts

Index